THE CHRYSOSTOM BIBLE
A Commentary Series for Preaching and Teaching
Philippians: A Commentary

THE CHRYSOSTOM BIBLE
A Commentary Series for Preaching and Teaching

Philippians: A Commentary

Paul Nadim Tarazi

OCABS PRESS
ST PAUL, MINNESOTA 55112
2009

THE CHRYSOSTOM BIBLE
PHILIPPIANS: A COMMENTARY

Other Books by the Author

I Thessalonians: A Commentary

Galatians: A Commentary

The Old Testament: An Introduction

Volume 1: Historical Traditions, revised edition

Volume 2: Prophetic Traditions

Volume 3: Psalms and Wisdom

The New Testament: An Introduction

Volume 1: Paul and Mark

Volume 2: Luke and Acts

Volume 3: Johannine Writings

Volume 4: Matthew and the Canon

The Chrysostom Bible
Genesis: A Commentary

Land and Covenant

The Chrysostom Bible
Philippians: A Commentary

ISBN 1-60191-010-X

Published by OCABS Press, St. Paul, Minnesota.
Printed in the United States of America.

Books are available through OCABS Press at special discounts for bulk purchases in the United States by academic institutions, churches, and other organizations. For more information please email OCABS Press at press@ocabs.org.

Abbreviations

Books by the Author

1 Thess   *1 Thessalonians: A Commentary,* Crestwood, NY: St. Vladimir's Seminary Press, 1982

Gal   *Galatians: A Commentary,* Crestwood, NY: St. Vladimir's Seminary Press, 1994

OTI_1 *The Old Testament: An Introduction, Volume 1: Historical Traditions,* revised edition, Crestwood, NY: St. Vladimir's Seminary Press, 2003

OTI_2 *The Old Testament: An Introduction, Volume 2: Prophetic Traditions,* Crestwood, NY: St. Vladimir's Seminary Press, 1994

OTI_3 *The Old Testament: An Introduction, Volume 3: Psalms and Wisdom,* Crestwood, NY: St. Vladimir's Seminary Press, 1996

NTI_1 *The New Testament: An Introduction, Volume 1: Paul and Mark,* Crestwood, NY: St. Vladimir's Seminary Press, 1999

NTI_2 *The New Testament: An Introduction, Volume 2: Luke and Acts,* Crestwood, NY: St. Vladimir's Seminary Press, 2001

NTI_3 *The New Testament: An Introduction, Volume 3: Johannine Writings,* Crestwood, NY: St. Vladimir's Seminary Press, 2004

NTI_4 *The New Testament: An Introduction, Volume 4: Matthew and the Canon,* St. Paul, MN: OCABS Press, 2009

C-Gen   *The Chrysostom Bible - Genesis: A Commentary,* St. Paul, MN: OCABS Press, 2009

LAC   *Land and Covenant,* St. Paul, MN: OCABS Press, 2009

Abbreviations

Books of the Old Testament*

Gen	Genesis	Job	Job	Hab	Habakkuk	
Ex	Exodus	Ps	Psalms	Zeph	Zephaniah	
Lev	Leviticus	Prov	Proverbs	Hag	Haggai	
Num	Numbers	Eccl	Ecclesiastes	Zech	Zechariah	
Deut	Deuteronomy	Song	Song of Solomon	Mal	Malachi	
Josh	Joshua	Is	Isaiah	Tob	Tobit	
Judg	Judges	Jer	Jeremiah	Jdt	Judith	
Ruth	Ruth	Lam	Lamentations	Wis	Wisdom	
1 Sam	1 Samuel	Ezek	Ezekiel	Sir	Sirach (Ecclesiasticus)	
2 Sam	2 Samuel	Dan	Daniel	Bar	Baruch	
1 Kg	1 Kings	Hos	Hosea	1 Esd	1 Esdras	
2 Kg	2 Kings	Joel	Joel	2 Esd	2 Esdras	
1 Chr	1 Chronicles	Am	Amos	1 Macc	1 Maccabees	
2 Chr	2 Chronicles	Ob	Obadiah	2 Macc	2 Maccabees	
Ezra	Ezra	Jon	Jonah	3 Macc	3 Maccabees	
Neh	Nehemiah	Mic	Micah	4 Macc	4 Maccabees	
Esth	Esther	Nah	Nahum			

Books of the New Testament

Mt	Matthew	Eph	Ephesians	Heb	Hebrews
Mk	Mark	Phil	Philippians	Jas	James
Lk	Luke	Col	Colossians	1 Pet	1 Peter
Jn	John	1 Thess	1 Thessalonians	2 Pet	2 Peter
Acts	Acts	2 Thess	2 Thessalonians	1 Jn	1 John
Rom	Romans	1 Tim	1 Timothy	2 Jn	2 John
1 Cor	1 Corinthians	2 Tim	2 Timothy	3 Jn	3 John
2 Cor	2 Corinthians	Titus	Titus	Jude	Jude
Gal	Galatians	Philem	Philemon	Rev	Revelation

Following the larger canon known as the Septuagint.

Contents

Preface

The present Bible Commentary Series is not so much in honor of John Chrysostom as it is to continue and promote his legacy as an interpreter of the biblical texts for preaching and teaching God's congregation, in order to prod its members to proceed on the way they started when they accepted God's calling. Chrysostom's virtual uniqueness is that he did not subscribe to any hermeneutic or methodology, since this would amount to introducing an extra-textual authority over the biblical texts. For him, scripture is its own interpreter. Listening to the texts time and again allowed him to realize that "call" and "read (aloud)" are not interconnected realities; rather, they are one reality since they both are renditions of the same Hebrew verb *qara'*. Given that words read aloud are words of instruction for one "to do them," the only valid reaction would be to hear, listen, obey, and abide by these words. All these connotations are subsumed in the same Hebrew verb *šama'*. On the other hand, these scriptural "words of life" are presented as readily understandable utterances of a father to his children (Isaiah 1:2-3). The recipients are never asked to engage in an intellectual debate with their divine instructor, or even among themselves, to fathom what he is saying. The Apostle to the Gentiles followed in the footsteps of the Prophets to Israel by handing down to them the Gospel, that is, the Law of God's Spirit through his Christ (Romans 8:2; Galatians 6:2) as fatherly instruction (1 Corinthians 4:15). He in turn wrote readily understandable letters to be read aloud. It is in these same footsteps that Chrysostom followed, having learned from both the Prophets and Paul that the same "words of life" carry also the sentence of death at the hand of the scriptural God, Judge of all

(Deuteronomy 28; Joshua 8:32-35; Psalm 82; Matthew 3:4-12; Romans 2:12-16; 1 Corinthians 10:1-11; Revelation 20:11-15).

While theological debates and hermeneutical theories come and go after having fed their proponents and their fans with passing human glory, the Golden Mouth's expository homilies, through the centuries, fed and still feed myriads of believers in so many traditions and countries. Virtually banned from dogmatic treatises, he survives in the hearts of "those who have ears to hear." His success is due to his commitment to exegesis rather than to futile hermeneutics. The latter behaves as someone who dictates on a living organism what it is supposed to be, whereas exegesis submits to that organism and endeavors to decipher it through trial and error. There is as much a far cry between the text and the theories about it as there is between a living organism and the theories about it. The biblical texts are the reality of God imparted through their being read aloud in the midst of the congregation, disregarding the value of the sermon that follows. The sermon, much less a theological treatise, is at best an invitation to hear and obey the text. Assessing the shape of an invitation card has no value whatsoever when it comes to the dinner itself; the guests are fed by the dinner, not by the invitation or its phrasing (Luke 14:16-24; Matthew 22:1-14).

This commentary series does not intend to promote Chrysostom's ideas as a public relation manager would do, but rather to follow in the footsteps of his approach as true children and heirs are expected to do. He used all the contemporary tools at his disposal to communicate God's written instruction to his hearers, as a doctor would with his patients, without spending unnecessary energy on peripheral debates requiring the use of professional jargon incomprehensible to the commoner. The writers of this series will try to do the same: muster to the best of their ability all necessary contemporary knowledge to communicate to the general readers the biblical message without burdening them with data unnecessary for that purpose. Whenever it will be deemed necessary or even helpful to do so, and in order to curtail burdensome and lengthy technical asides within the commentaries, specialized monographs related either to specific topics or to the scriptural background—literary, socio-political, or archeological—will be issued as companions to the series.

Paul Nadim Tarazi
Editor

Introduction

This Introduction is unconventional. Instead of approaching the text as a document for personal study in order to figure out its meaning and then elaborate on it, I shall concentrate on using it according to its own literary fabric. One might ask, "What is the difference? Is not any text literature after all?" Yes, indeed it is, in the sense that it is made out of letters (*literae* in Latin) and words. However, not every text functions in the same way. One basic difference between texts lies in their audience. Some texts are intended for a specific audience and are usually to be "studied" and "debated" by those who are both interested and capable to pursue such tasks. Others texts are "public" and thus "open" in the sense that they are written essentially to be immediately heard. The assumption then must be that they are readily understandable and, consequently, non debatable. They are either to be *readily* accepted or refused but, at any rate, not analyzed. If so, then they must be at the lowest possible common denominator of understanding. On the other hand, if such texts were merely informational, they would not make sense since the hearer would not be getting anything practically or theoretically, especially if the recipient is not allowed any analysis or debate. They would make sense only if they are instructional in a double sense: an instruction to be understood *and* to be followed, that is, a commandment. If so, then such texts are meant to be heard in the double sense of that verb: to be received and to be hearkened to.[1]

---

[1] The Hebrew verb *šama'* and its Greek counterpart *akouō* bear this double connotation just as often as the English "hear." The Greek also uses the cognate *hypakouō* which has the specific meaning of "obey." The understanding is assumed

This is precisely how the biblical texts present themselves. Let us hear, for instance, the impressive divine injunction to the prophet Ezekiel:

And he [the Lord] said to me: "Son of man, I send you to the people of Israel, to a nation of rebels, who have rebelled against me; they and their fathers have transgressed against me to this very day. The people also are impudent and stubborn: I send you to them; and you shall say to them, 'Thus says the Lord God.' And whether they hear or refuse to hear (for they are a rebellious house) they will know that there has been a prophet among them. And you, son of man, be not afraid of them, nor be afraid of their words, though briers and thorns are with you and you sit upon scorpions; be not afraid of their words, nor be dismayed at their looks, for they are a rebellious house." (2:3-6)

And he said to me: "Son of man, go, get you to the house of Israel, and speak with my words to them. For you are not sent to a people of foreign speech and a hard language, but to the house of Israel—not to many peoples of foreign speech and a hard language, whose words you cannot understand. Surely, if I sent you to such, they would listen to you. But the house of Israel will not listen to you; for they are not willing to listen to me; because all the house of Israel are of a hard forehead and of a stubborn heart." (3:4-7)

Moreover he said to me, "Son of man, all my words that I shall speak to you receive in your heart, and hear with your ears. And go, get you to the exiles, to your people, and say to them, 'Thus says the Lord God'; whether they hear or refuse to hear." (3:10-11)

---

since the intention is that the instructions be obeyed; hence, the necessity of the lowest possible common denominator in their phraseology and presentation.

Two things are very clear: (1) the message is readily understandable; (2) it is a message that is intended to be heeded. There is no room for analysis and debate as though the text were a thesis to be proven or defended. Still the question that remains is, "What is the basis for such an absolute authoritative stand?"[2] To answer by referring to a philosophical Almighty God who can do whatever he wills is begging the question, since one would first need to prove his existence, which is repeatedly shown to be a futile endeavor; and even if one were able to do so, what is the proof that this is precisely what he wills? Moreover, to try to find a premise outside the text would open the door for debate regarding the premise itself and its validity. Besides, such an approach would rob the text of its authority, since it would need a prop from outside. This, in turn, would mean that we would be not hearing the text itself, but reading into it.

The only way out of this dilemma is to inquire from the text itself. The answer is actually readily available when one realizes that the text is *not* a compendium of formulas and statements about a "subject matter" that is "out there," existing before and independently of the text and that was incorporated into the text in diverse manners ranging from childish stories to more sophisticated utterances.[3] The text itself is a narrative *through time* since it spans generations: notice Ezekiel's "they *and their fathers* have transgressed against me to this very day," and the rebellious addressees are not the "fathers" whose city was

---

[2] This is not the same as saying the commandments are autocratically imposed through the medium of physical power and oppression; if such were the case, then they cannot be "refused."

[3] If it were so, then one wonders if the text is necessary at all. In actuality, the wide range of "theologies" does show that the biblical text is manipulated rather than heard, let alone hearkened to. Every theologian reads into the text his premise, which then becomes a magical hermeneutical key to unlocking and understanding the entire Bible.

destroyed, but the younger generation living in the land of exile as a consequence of God's punishing their fathers' city. That this is not a passing remark in Ezekiel is borne out by the three extensive and repetitious "narratives" (in chs. 16, 20 and 23) which are central to the message of the prophet and which extend the lineage of the fathers to the times of the oppression in Egypt (Ezek 20:6-10). Consequently, for the text to be a narrative, it has (1) to have a beginning and an end, and (2) to follow a thread that holds it together and thus makes it "credible," that is to say, makes sense of the movement between *that* beginning and *that* end. The choice of these three Ezekelian chapters is actually very much à *propos* since they form, in a nutshell, the narrative line of the expanded biblical "story" stretching from Genesis or Exodus until 2 Kings. In both cases, the beginning is an act of unexplainable magnanimity on the part of a God toward a people that kept proving itself unworthy of such generosity and kept repaying that God with unimaginable ungratefulness, not found even among nations whose deities did much less for them (Jer 2:9-13). At the end, after having multiplied his gracious visitations, God had no choice except to visit his people with the punishment of destruction and exile.

It is worth digressing here in order to explain the statement "God had no choice except to act in a given way." Such may sound hard to accept for people who have been indoctrinated into viewing and thus defining God as an Almighty Being who is not bound by anything and can do whatever he wills. This was not the view of deities in the Ancient Near East. The basic function, and thus definition, of a deity was that of a judge. If a deity ceased to be a judge, and assumedly an equitable one, then it lost all its divine attributes and prerogatives. This reality is summed up in Psalm 82:

A Psalm of Asaph. God has taken his place in the divine council; in the midst of the gods he holds judgment: "How long will you judge unjustly and show partiality to the wicked? Selah Give justice to the weak and the fatherless; maintain the right of the afflicted and the destitute. Rescue the weak and the needy; deliver them from the hand of the wicked." They have neither knowledge nor understanding, they walk about in darkness; all the foundations of the earth are shaken. I say, "You are gods, sons of the Most High, all of you; nevertheless, you shall die like men, and fall like any prince." Arise, O God, judge the earth; for to thee belong all the nations!

It is clear then that the biblical God is not the only God, in a philosophical, ontological sense, but rather the only *true* God in a real, functional sense. He *alone* among the gods acts as he is supposed to act: as an equitable judge.[4] Judging is his duty without which he would not be *truly* (that is, de facto)[5] what he is (supposed or expected to be). This explains his reasoning in the following passage of Ezekiel:

Have I any pleasure in the death of the wicked, says the Lord God, and not rather that he should turn from his way and live? But when a righteous man turns away from his righteousness and commits iniquity and does the same abominable things that the wicked man does, shall he live? None of the righteous deeds which he has done shall be remembered; for the treachery of which he is guilty and the sin he has committed, he shall die. Yet you say, "The way of the Lord is not just." Hear now, O house of Israel: Is my way not just? Is it not your ways that are not just? When a righteous man turns away from his righteousness and commits iniquity, he shall die for it; for the iniquity which he has committed he shall die. Again, when a wicked man turns away

---

[4] See further Ps 96:13; 97:2, 6; 98:9; 99:4.
[5] This is actually the meaning of the Hebrew *'emet*.

from the wickedness he has committed and does what is lawful
and right, he shall save his life. Because he considered and turned
away from all the transgressions which he had committed, he shall
surely live, he shall not die. Yet the house of Israel says, "The way
of the Lord is not just." O house of Israel, are my ways not just? Is
it not your ways that are not just? Therefore I will judge you, O
house of Israel, every one according to his ways, says the Lord
God. Repent and turn from all your transgressions, lest iniquity be
your ruin. Cast away from you all the transgressions which you
have committed against me, and get yourselves a new heart and a
new spirit! Why will you die, O house of Israel? For I have no
pleasure in the death of any one, says the Lord God; so turn, and
live. (18:23-32)

And the crux of the matter lies in that were he not a judge, and
again assumedly an equitable one, then there would be no hope
for all of us, as Paul reasons, along the same premise as Ezekiel:

Then what advantage has the Jew? Or what is the value of
circumcision? Much in every way. To begin with, the Jews are
entrusted with the oracles of God. What if some were unfaithful?
Does their faithlessness nullify the faithfulness of God? By no
means! Let God be *true* though every man be false, as it is written,
"That thou mayest be justified in thy words, and prevail when
thou art judged." But if our wickedness serves to show the justice
of God, what shall we say? *That God is unjust to inflict wrath on us?*
(I speak in a human way.) By no means! *For then how could God
judge the world?* (Rom 3:1-6)

But then, why does the biblical story not end with the divine
punishment? Again, to answer from a philosophical premise
grounded in a given understanding of God as being almighty at
will or ethically good, or being the expression of ultimate
goodness, is to fall into *eisegesis*: reading the text in the light of a
foreign premise. A judge is not to act willfully or, for that matter,

be "good" as opposed to being "evil," character wise. A judge is by definition neither willful, nor good or evil. He is bound to be just; otherwise he would not be a judge. For him to act willfully, or to try to be "good," may affect his verdict and ultimately his being a judge. And, if so, to plagiarize Paul, "how could he judge" and maintain the world he has established? For indeed:

> Say among the nations, "The Lord reigns! Yea, the world is established, it shall never be moved; he will judge the peoples with equity.[6]" Let the heavens be glad, and let the earth rejoice; let the sea roar, and all that fills it; let the field exult, and everything in it! Then shall all the trees of the wood sing for joy before the Lord, for he comes, for he comes to judge the earth. He will judge the world with righteousness, and the peoples with his truth. (Ps 96:10-13)

Even more, a judge, as judge, is actually above ethics. He produces the good and the evil in the sense that his just verdict will be good for the one found innocent and bad for the one found guilty. Were the judge not capable of producing either good or evil, his judgment would not be effective since he would not be in control of the situation and his world. This is precisely how God presents himself in the Bible: "I form light and create darkness, I make weal and create woe, I am the Lord, who do all these things." (Is 45:7)[7] Again, the clue to finding the meaning of this statement has to lie in the immediate background of the text, the Ancient Near East. Besides being the judge of his people, a god was also the father of that people, the one who reared them and took care of their needs. Notice God's opening statement in Isaiah as preamble to his harsh verdict: "Hear, O

---

[6] From the root *yašar* (upright).

[7] One can imagine how this text would create havoc, as it actually did over the centuries, if it were handled on Gnostic philosophical terms. It would a basis for God being (ontologically) good and evil at will!

heavens, and give ear, O earth; for the Lord has spoken: 'Sons
have I reared and brought up, but they have rebelled against me.
The ox knows its owner, and the ass its master's crib; but Israel
does not know, my people does not understand.'" (1:2-3) Notice
also the confession of the repentant people in the same book:
"For thou art our Father, though Abraham does not know us
and Israel does not acknowledge us; thou, O Lord, art our
Father, our Redeemer from of old is thy name." (63:16) Still, by
itself the deity's "fatherhood" does not explain why God, who is
also and essentially a judge, had a way out in not allowing the
story to end with his verdict of condemnation, without
jeopardizing his justice. In order to find the valid and
appropriate explanation one must look into another basic aspect
of Ancient Near Eastern reality, which plays a paramount role in
the biblical narrative, namely that deities ruled through the
intermediacy of their appointed monarchs.

By the mere fact that the king was seated on the divine throne,
he himself was functionally divine in the sense that he
represented his god and thus had to act on the latter's behalf.
Anything less than divine behavior on the part of the king, while
seated on the throne of righteousness and justice, would be
jeopardizing his god's status and thus tantamount to committing
the ultimate blasphemy: allowing the name of the deity to be
mocked. The king is referred to as "god" in Psalm 45: "Your
throne, O God, endures for ever and ever. Your royal scepter is a
scepter of equity; you love righteousness and hate wickedness.
Therefore God, your God, has anointed you with the oil of
gladness above your fellows." (vv.6-7) Also the divine titles of
"god" and "father" appear in the royal protocol: "For to us a
child is born, to us a son is given; and the government will be
upon his shoulder, and his name will be called 'Wonderful
Counselor, Mighty God, Everlasting Father, Prince of Peace.' Of

the increase of his government and of peace there will be no end, upon the throne of David, and over his kingdom, to establish it, and to uphold it with justice and with righteousness from this time forth and for evermore." (Is 9:6-7) On the other hand, given his divine status, the king had full responsibility as well as full power; consequently, he would get all the glory if his realm was prosperous or victorious against the enemies and, conversely, he would be accountable for any mismanagement and its aftermath. Such is made very clear in the Prophets as well as in the Books of Samuel and Kings, where the kings and the entire leadership are singled out for the blame. To be sure, all the people are also punished for the sin of their leader in the same way as an army or a city suffers loss for the mistake of its general or its monarch, respectively. The king can be fully cut off from the ruling office either literally, through death, or through the demise of his dynasty. The people, however, are usually never totally obliterated: the survivors either are exiled or remain where they are under foreign rule, no longer in control of their destiny as an entity. Put otherwise, the king ceases to be a ruler and suffers a change in his functionality, whereas the individual basically remains what he was before, under the rule of someone else.[8]

Putting the burden on the king and the leaders of the people allowed the Prophets to extend the end beyond the end of a kingship and a city. However, in order to keep matters in perspective and not surmise that God was bound by the Prophets' hope but rather solely by what makes him God, his justice, they expressed their hope in the language of divine

---

[8] That is why, from the perspective of the Bible, the citizens of Judah or Israel under Solomon and the following kings were in a situation similar in kind to that in which their fathers fared under Pharaoh.

promise. Such language fits perfectly within the realm of the judge's authority. He can at any time decide to lessen the penalty imposed upon the guilty; usually this is done either because the condemned has shown remorse and started behaving in a becoming manner, or because the judge considers that the elapsed time of penalty is enough and he decides to give another chance to the condemned. The latter would be an act of sheer mercy, and it is the path followed by the biblical prophetic teaching. However, in this case, the mercy is conditional in the sense that the one who was given another chance is to show fruits of one's repentance according to the conditions and rules of behavior imposed by the merciful judge. A classic text for the above is found in Ezekiel:

> Thus says the Lord God: I will gather you from the peoples, and assemble you out of the countries where you have been scattered, and I will give you the land of Israel. And when they come there, they will remove from it all its detestable things and all its abominations. And I will give them one heart, and put a new spirit within them; I will take the stony heart out of their flesh and give them a heart of flesh, that they may walk in my statutes and keep my ordinances and obey them; and they shall be my people, and I will be their God. But as for those whose heart goes after their detestable things and their abominations, I will requite their deeds upon their own heads, says the Lord God. (11:17-21)

The new spirit and new heart are none other than those God has been requiring from the people all along so that they would not fall under his condemnation (18:23-32 quoted above). The forgiven people, then, are not free to do their own will, but

---

[9] See, e.g., Is 40:1-2 (Comfort, comfort my people, says your God. Speak tenderly to Jerusalem, and cry to her that her warfare is ended, that her iniquity is pardoned, that she has received from the Lord's hand double for all her sins.)

rather to abide by the same statutes and ordinances they had broken thereby losing their life and liberty. Lest they forget this matter and fall in the sin of arrogance, which was the reason for their demise, the third and final Ezekelian passage referring to the new spirit and the new heart makes it clear that the new state of affairs will have as a result concomitantly the glorification of the merciful judge and the constant reminder to the people of their past shameful actions that had forced the judge's hand in punishing them:

A new heart I will give you, and a new spirit I will put within you; and I will take out of your flesh the heart of stone and give you a heart of flesh. And I will put my spirit within you, and cause you to walk in my statutes and be careful to observe my ordinances. You shall dwell in the land which I gave to your fathers; and you shall be my people, and I will be your God … Then you will remember your evil ways, and your deeds that were not good; and you will loathe yourselves for your iniquities and your abominable deeds. It is not for your sake that I will act, says the Lord God; let that be known to you. Be ashamed and confounded for your ways, O house of Israel. Thus says the Lord God: On the day that I cleanse you from all your iniquities, I will cause the cities to be inhabited, and the waste places shall be rebuilt. And the land that was desolate shall be tilled, instead of being the desolation that it was in the sight of all who passed by. And they will say, "This land that was desolate has become like the garden of Eden; and the waste and desolate and ruined cities are now inhabited and fortified." Then the nations that are left round about you shall know that I, the Lord, have rebuilt the ruined places, and replanted that which was desolate; I, the Lord, have spoken, and I will do it. (36:26-28, 31-36)

It is precisely this chronological story "line" that forms the thread of the biblical narrative consigned in the Law and the Prophets. The ultimate beginning starts with God, who for no apparent reason from our perspective, established the world on a sane (viable, as it is supposed to be)[10] basis and settled the human being in a garden with all the necessary ingredients for that being to conduct a sane (healthy, viable, as it is supposed to be)[11] life until his demise, since after all "the Lord God formed man of dust from the ground" (Gen 2:7) and "you are dust, and to dust you shall return" (3:19). This original state of viability is not to be taken for granted since it is ensured solely by God's will and action. The Hebrew verb *bara'* with which the biblical narrative opens (Gen 1:1) means "render healthy, sane, viable." This explains why this divine action takes place against the odds of destruction (represented by the threatening darkness and the raging waters)[12] and desolation (*tohu wabohu*).[13] The same applies to the human being who has to acknowledge that his life in the setting where everything is provided for him to live, a garden watered and yet never threatened by the four mighty rivers that flow through it (2:10-14), was conditional and depended on his abiding by God's will, i.e., according to his command: "And the Lord God *commanded* the man, saying, 'You may freely eat of every tree of the garden; but of the tree of the knowledge of good and evil you shall not eat, for in the day that you eat of it you shall die.'" (vv.16-17) When man contravened God's commandment, it is God who, as a judge, implemented the verdict: "And to Adam he said, 'Because you

---

[10] This is the meaning of the Hebrew *šalem*; consequently the peace (sanity, *šalom*) is the original status of things.

[11] See previous note. This view expressed in the story of the forming of man in Gen 2 is in conformity with that found in the story of the creation of the world in Gen 1.

[12] Notice how, in the narrative, both these elements are not God's work. His work, actually, consists in wrenching out of them the light and dry land, which are the actual "world" of the earthly flora and fauna as well as of the human being, an earthly mammal.

[13] This expression is found in scripture to describe the situation of rubble in which a destroyed city and country find themselves (Is 24:10-12; 34:11; Jer 4:23-26).

have listened to the voice of your wife, and have eaten of the tree of which I commanded you, 'You shall not eat of it,' ... you are dust, and to dust you shall return.'" (3:14, 19)

However, instead of the total death of Adam, which would have eradicated humanity, God gives the latter a chance by exiling Adam. Still, the Adamic progeny did not fare better: "The Lord saw that the wickedness of man was great in the earth, and that every imagination of the thoughts of his heart was only evil continually. And the Lord was sorry that he had made man on the earth, and it grieved him to his heart. So the Lord said, 'I will blot out man whom I have created from the face of the ground, man and beast and creeping things and birds of the air, for I am sorry that I have made them.'" (6:5-7) But again, God was gracious and contained the destructive powers of the flood as a passing episode within the life span of Noah instead of allowing it to put an end to all life on earth: "These are the generations of Noah ... And Noah had three sons, Shem, Ham, and Japheth ... Noah was six hundred years old when the flood of waters came upon the earth ... After the flood Noah lived three hundred and fifty years. All the days of Noah were nine hundred and fifty years; and he died. These are the generations of the sons of Noah, Shem, Ham, and Japheth; sons were born to them after the flood." (6:9-10; 7:6; 9:28-10:1) However, this time, in order to ensure that the sins of the human beings would not affect his decision, God binds the latter to a unilateral covenantal commitment on his part: "This is the sign of the covenant which I make between me and you and every living creature that is with you, for all future generations: I set my bow in the cloud, and it shall be a sign of the covenant between me and the earth. When I bring clouds over the earth and the bow is seen in the clouds, I will remember my covenant which is between me and you and every living creature of all flesh; and the waters shall never again become a flood to destroy all flesh. When the bow is in the clouds, I will look upon it and remember the everlasting covenant between God and every living creature of all flesh that is upon the earth." (9:12-16) Yet again, humanity falls prey of its condemnable hubris (11:1-9).

Thus, the introductory story consigned in the first ten and a half chapters of Genesis ends on a very sour note. So God, we are told, decides to go a different route. This time round he picks up where he had ended the first time, with a promise (12:1-3) linked to a covenant (17:1-22), just as he did with Noah,[14] inaugurating a lengthy and much more complex overarching narrative defining the entire scripture of the Law and the Prophets. This narrative, which is the story of how God finally gains control of the situation in spite of the human being, starts with a covenant based on a promise and ends with a promise of an everlasting covenant. Between this beginning and that end lies, at the heart of the entire story, a third covenant which is bound to a set of instructions. Just as was the case with Adam, these instructions are meant to sustain life granted by God. By the same token, should man contravene them, death ensues as punishment. This conditional covenant, though apparently harsh when it is compared to the non-conditionality of the others, is actually the ultimate expression of God's gracefulness. It was the only way God could maintain his caring fatherhood toward us without jeopardizing what defines him as deity, his being judge.

---

[14] Notice the intended parallelism between Noah and Abraham: "Noah was a righteous man, *blameless in his generation; Noah walked with God* ... And God said to Noah ... '*I will establish my covenant with you*'" (6:9, 13, 18); "When Abram was ninety-nine years old the Lord appeared to Abram, and said to him, 'I am God Almighty; *walk before me, and be blameless. And I will make my covenant between me and you*, and will multiply you exceedingly.'" (17:1-2)

Let us analyze in more detail how this set of instructions, the *torah*, actually controls the entire narrative of the Law and the Prophets and, by the same token, functions as the expression of God's fatherly care and love for us. The stories of Abraham (Abram) the forefather and of Jacob-Israel, representing the hearers of the message, underscore the recurrence of the same sin throughout the generations: instead of awaiting the necessary bread from the divine father, each of them runs down to Egypt to secure that bread from strangers. This phraseology is clearly in view of what will be the main point of the *torah*:

All the commandment which I command you this day you shall be careful to do, that you may live and multiply, and go in and possess the land which the Lord swore to give to your fathers. And you shall remember all the way which the Lord your God has led you these forty years in the wilderness, that he might humble you, testing you to know what was in your heart, whether you would keep his commandments, or not. And he humbled you and let you hunger and fed you with manna, which you did not know, nor did your fathers know; that he might make you know that man does not live by bread alone, but that man lives by everything that proceeds out of the mouth of the Lord. (Deut 8:1-3)

Although Abram's mistake could have cost the life of Sarai (Sarah) and thus the existence of Jacob-Israel, God comes to the rescue immediately in order to show that he is capable of subduing his people's enemies at will. Abram's descent to Egypt, including his short stay there, is glossed over as an interlude during his sojourn at Bethel.[15] On the other hand, Jacob, who

---

[15] "Thence he removed to the mountain on the east of Bethel, and pitched his tent, with Bethel on the west and Ai on the east; and there he built an altar to the Lord and called on the name of the Lord. And Abram journeyed on, still going toward the Negeb. Now there was a famine in the land. So Abram went down to Egypt to sojourn there, for the famine was severe in the land ... So Abram went up from Egypt, he and

should have known better from the experience of his forefather, was punished for the same mistake with an exile of four hundred thirty years (Ex 12:40-41). Here, for the first time, we have the pattern, which I introduced earlier on the basis of Ezekiel's teaching, of splitting between the demise of the leader as the main culprit (Jacob dies in Egypt) and the preservation of the people in exile for an eventual restoration. Furthermore and more importantly, again following Ezekiel's lead, this second chance is not only bound to, but actually in view of "walking in God's statutes and observing his commandments." It is, indeed, very clear in the Book of Exodus that the exodus out of Egypt is not the main action of God, but rather it is done *with the aim* of getting the people to the divine mountain where God appears to Moses and commissions him to bring the people out of Egypt so that he, God, could inform them of his statutes and ordinances that would secure their preservation in the future. Put otherwise, were it not for the handing down of the *torah* there would have been no exodus or, at least, such exodus would have been meaningless since it would be oxymoronic that people would leave a place where bread abounds in order to end up condemned to death in a wilderness where nothing grows.

But the statutes and commandments found in Exodus, Leviticus, and Numbers, especially those linked to offerings of grains and livestock, are meant to be implemented in Canaan and not in the wilderness. When one hears the Pentateuch narrative, one gets the distinct impression that, while God was providing bread and water as the need arose in the wilderness,

---

his wife, and all that he had, and Lot with him, into the Negeb. Now Abram was very rich in cattle, in silver, and in gold. And he journeyed on from the Negeb as far as Bethel, to the place where his tent had been at the beginning, between Bethel and Ai, to the place where he had made an altar at the first; and there Abram called on the name of the Lord." (Gen 12:6-8; 13:1-4)

his main concern was to hand down to the people the "rules" for them to *keep* when in Canaan, the land of plenty, so that God would *keep* them and not shorten their days there by exiling them to another "Egypt."[16] Thus, in scripture, God's law is given with the following generations—and not the actual one—in mind when it comes to divine protection. The first generation, in whose times God's prophets spoke or his Law was given, is already doomed. This is at its clearest in the Pentateuchal narrative: the entire generation that left Egypt, including Moses, died before entering Canaan. In view of that, the Law was issued a second time in a *book*, Deuteronomy, to be preserved for the ages:

> These are the words of the covenant which the Lord commanded Moses to make with the people of Israel in the land of Moab, besides the covenant which he had made with them at Horeb ... And the Lord would single him out from all the tribes of Israel for calamity, in accordance with all the curses of the covenant written in this book of the law ... And Moses wrote this law, and gave it to the priests the sons of Levi, who carried the ark of the covenant of the Lord, and to all the elders of Israel ... When Moses had finished writing the words of this law in a book, to the very end, Moses commanded the Levites who carried the ark of the

---

[16] There is definitely in scripture a recurring play on the use of the verb *šamar* (keep) in both directions: the people are to keep God's law for him to be indeed their God and thus keep them. Actually, as we heard earlier in Ezekiel, it is only then that they are his people and he is their God: "I will take the stony heart out of their flesh and give them a heart of flesh, that they may walk in my statutes and keep my ordinances and obey them; and they shall be my people, and I will be their God. But as for those whose heart goes after their detestable things and their abominations, I will requite their deeds upon their own heads, says the Lord God" (11:19-21); "A new heart I will give you, and a new spirit I will put within you; and I will take out of your flesh the heart of stone and give you a heart of flesh. And I will put my spirit within you, and cause you to walk in my statutes and be careful to observe my ordinances. You shall dwell in the land which I gave to your fathers; and you shall be my people, and I will be your God." (36:26-28)

covenant of the Lord, "Take this book of the law, and put it by
the side of the ark of the covenant of the Lord your God, that it
may be there for a witness against you" ... And when he [the king]
sits on the throne of his kingdom, he shall write for himself in a
book a copy of this law (*mišneh hattorah, deuteronomion*) from that
which is in the charge of the Levitical priests; and it shall be with
him, and he shall read in it all the days of his life, that he may
learn to fear the Lord his God, by keeping all the words of this law
and these statutes, and doing them; that his heart may not be
lifted up above his brethren, and that he may not turn aside from
the commandment, either to the right hand or to the left; so that
he may continue long in his kingdom, he and his children, in
Israel. (29:1, 21; 31:9, 24-26; 17:18-20)

Joshua, Moses' minister, whose name means "the Lord saves,"
will lead God's people into Canaan not as a general—this role
will be incumbent on the commander of the army of the Lord
(Josh 5:13-15)—but as someone who was commissioned in these
words:

No man shall be able to stand before you all the days of your life;
as I was with Moses, so I will be with you; I will not fail you or
forsake you. Be strong and of good courage; for you shall cause
this people to inherit the land which I swore to their fathers to
give them. Only be strong and very courageous, being careful to
do according to all the law which Moses my servant commanded
you; turn not from it to the right hand or to the left, that you may
have good success wherever you go. This book of the law shall not
depart out of your mouth, but you shall meditate on it day and
night, that you may be careful to do according to all that is written
in it; for then you shall make your way prosperous, and then you
shall have good success. Have I not commanded you? Be strong
and of good courage; be not frightened, neither be dismayed; for
the Lord your God is with you wherever you go. (Josh 1:5-9)

What Joshua and his elders abided by all the days of their lives was soon forgotten: at their death, the people forsook the Lord's commandments (Josh 24:31; Judg 2:7-13). Yet, the Lord refrained from implementing his just and justified wrath announced in the Law. The reason is, as Ezekiel clearly stated, that the Lord be ultimately shown a just judge when he ultimately condemns. This is precisely what Paul underscored:

> Do you suppose, O man, that when you judge those who do such things and yet do them yourself, you will escape the judgment of God? Or do you presume upon the riches of his kindness and forbearance and patience? Do you not know that God's kindness is meant to lead you to repentance? But by your hard and impenitent heart you are storing up wrath for yourself on the day of wrath when God's righteous judgment will be revealed ... Then what advantage has the Jew? Or what is the value of circumcision? Much in every way. To begin with, the Jews are entrusted with the oracles of God. What if some were unfaithful? Does their faithlessness nullify the faithfulness of God? By no means! Let God be true though every man be false, as it is written, "That thou mayest be justified in thy words, and prevail when thou art judged." But if our wickedness serves to show the justice of God, what shall we say? That God is unjust to inflict wrath on us? (I speak in a human way.) By no means! For then how could God judge the world? (Rom 2:3-5; 3:1-6)

This divine forbearance is actually reflected in the biblical narrative itself. The period of the Judges amounts to four hundred twenty years, the same as the sojourn in Egypt. Again, according to the narrative, a similar time period elapses under the kings of Israel and Judah until the fall of Jerusalem and its temple in 587 B.C. This means that, before God released his wrath, he waited double the amount of time Israel sojourned in Egypt due to Jacob's sin. The message cannot be clearer: God, who delivered as a father would, is now rightfully intervening as the just judge. Thus, all the following generations ended up not being better than the first one who received the Law: they, each in turn, had the Law and yet did not abide by it. Now that the message is clear, God, in his mercy, intervenes for the third and final time, biblically speaking, and gives his people the last chance, which is also the last chance for all nations (see especially Is 40-66). However, since this last chance is offered by the same God, it is again, and this time very clearly, tied to his law and the people's abiding by it. What Ezekiel taught, is underscored in Isaiah 40-55 where this message, being the last chance, is made universal: God's law will be taught not only to Israel but also to all nations, who will have to abide by it and walk in its light, lest it consumes them as fire (Is 2). That this chance is indeed the last can be seen in that the end of the line is not a restored Jerusalem, but the heavenly one (Is 56-66) where Gentiles as well as Israel will be serving the Lord on an equal footing and always reminded of God's wrath spoken of in his law:

> Rejoice with Jerusalem, and be glad for her, all you who love her; rejoice with her in joy, all you who mourn over her; that you may suck and be satisfied with her consoling breasts; that you may drink deeply with delight from the abundance of her glory. For thus says the Lord: Behold, I will extend prosperity to her like a river, and the wealth of the nations like an overflowing stream; and you shall suck, you shall be carried upon her hip, and dandled upon her knees. As one whom his mother comforts, so I will comfort you; you shall be comforted in Jerusalem. You shall see, and your heart shall rejoice; your bones shall flourish like the grass; and it shall be known that the hand of the Lord is with his servants, and his indignation is against his enemies. For behold, the Lord will come in fire, and his chariots like the stormwind, to render his anger in fury, and his rebuke with flames of fire. For by fire will the Lord execute judgment, and by his sword, upon all

flesh; and those slain by the Lord shall be many. Those who sanctify and purify themselves to go into the gardens, following one in the midst, eating swine's flesh and the abomination and mice, shall come to an end together, says the Lord. For I know their works and their thoughts, and I am coming to gather all nations and tongues; and they shall come and shall see my glory, and I will set a sign among them. And from them I will send survivors to the nations, to Tarshish, Put, and Lud, who draw the bow, to Tubal and Javan, to the coastlands afar off, that have not heard my fame or seen my glory; and they shall declare my glory among the nations. And they shall bring all your brethren from all the nations as an offering to the Lord, upon horses, and in chariots, and in litters, and upon mules, and upon dromedaries, to my holy mountain Jerusalem, says the Lord, just as the Israelites bring their cereal offering in a clean vessel to the house of the Lord. And some of them also I will take for priests and for Levites, says the Lord. For as the new heavens and the new earth which I will make shall remain before me, says the Lord; so shall your descendants and your name remain. From new moon to new moon, and from sabbath to sabbath, all flesh shall come to worship before me, says the Lord. And they shall go forth and look on the dead bodies of the men that have rebelled against me; for their worm shall not die, their fire shall not be quenched, and they shall be an abhorrence to all flesh. (Is 66:10-24)

The significance of this last point lies in that it is not peculiar to Isaiah. It is actually shared by the Scroll of the Twelve Prophets, which is a counterpart to Isaiah. They both have a parallel structure: both span the entire "story" of the kingdoms of Samaria and Jerusalem, their destruction, the exile, and the post-exilic period.[17] At the end of Malachi we have a passage where

---

[17] Actually the Latter Prophets (Isaiah, Jeremiah, Ezekiel, and the Twelve Prophets) form an *inclusio*: the two comprehensive stories sandwich Jeremiah and Ezekiel who deal specifically with the fall of Jerusalem, the former from within its walls and the latter from the land of its exile.

the hearer is actually thrown into a situation similar to that extant at the end of Deuteronomy—the last book of the Law—with an invitation to listen to Moses' followers:

> For behold, the day comes, burning like an oven, when all the arrogant and all evildoers will be stubble; the day that comes shall burn them up, says the Lord of hosts, so that it will leave them neither root nor branch. But for you who fear my name the sun of righteousness shall rise, with healing in its wings. You shall go forth leaping like calves from the stall. And you shall tread down the wicked, for they will be ashes under the soles of your feet, on the day when I act, says the Lord of hosts. Remember the law of my servant Moses, the statutes and ordinances that I commanded him at Horeb for all Israel. Behold, I will send you Elijah the prophet before the great and terrible day of the Lord comes. And he will turn the hearts of fathers to their children and the hearts of children to their fathers, lest I come and smite the land with a curse. (Mal 4:1-6)

Both these aspects, God's unconditional mercy, expressed in his everlasting covenant,[18] and the way to keep oneself within it, by abiding in his will embedded in a written Law,[19] are clearly reflected in two features of the teaching of Ezekiel and Second-Isaiah (Is 40-55). The centrality of the Law in that period of the last chance can be seen in the prominence of the sabbath in Ezekiel, which speaks to the exiles in view of the post-exilic period, and Third-Isaiah (Is 56-66) whose setting and concern is the post-exilic situation. With the exception of Hosea 2:11, Amos 8:5, Isaiah 1:13, and Jeremiah 17:21-27, the occurrences of "sabbath" are confined in the Prophetic Books to Ezekiel (20:12, 13, 16, 20, 21, 24: 22:8, 26; 23:38; 44:24; 45:17; 46:1,

---

[18] See, e.g., Is 55:3; 61:8; Ezek 16:60; 37:26.

[19] Notice how the new Law of the new everlasting covenant (Jer 32:40) will be "written" on their hearts (Jer 31:33).

3, 4, 12) and Third-Isaiah (Is 56:2, 4, 6; 58:13; 66:23). The whole purpose of the institution of the sabbath is to secure in the mind of the people an everlasting remembrance that it is God's everlasting word embedded in the words of the Law, which makes them who they are—God's people—and sustains them in the same way as bread sustains human life. In other words, the people gather on the sabbath day in order to recall that the divine commandments, which are inscribed once and for all ages in the Law and which each of the previous generations disobeyed, are still valid "this day," as Deuteronomy repeatedly underscores, and are delivered to the hearers in order to be obeyed. However, to make it clear to the hearers that this is indeed the last chance after which comes God's final judgment, Second-Isaiah likens this last covenant to the Abrahamic, and beyond it the Noachic, covenants where it is God's mercy and unilateral commitment that are brought out (Is 51:1-2 and 54:1-10). Since both of these covenants are inclusive (Noah is the father of the post-diluvial humanity and Abraham's covenantal tent encompasses any and every one "born in your house, or bought with your money from any foreigner who is not of your offspring"), the final horizon is the Adamic garden of Eden (Is 51:3; Ezek 35:36). Yet again, each one is to live by the righteousness required by the everlasting Law; the righteousness of others will not help as was the case in Abraham's times (Gen 18:20-33):

> Son of man, when a land sins against me by acting faithlessly, and I stretch out my hand against it, and break its staff of bread and send famine upon it, and cut off from it man and beast, even if these three men, Noah, Daniel, and Job, were in it, they would deliver but their own lives by their righteousness, says the Lord God. If I cause wild beasts to pass through the land, and they ravage it, and it be made desolate, so that no man may pass

through because of the beasts; even if these three men were in it, as I live, says the Lord God, they would deliver neither sons nor daughters; they alone would be delivered, but the land would be desolate. Or if I bring a sword upon that land, and say, Let a sword go through the land; and I cut off from it man and beast; though these three men were in it, as I live, says the Lord God, they would deliver neither sons nor daughters, but they alone would be delivered. Or if I send a pestilence into that land, and pour out my wrath upon it with blood, to cut off from it man and beast; even if Noah, Daniel, and Job were in it, as I live, says the Lord God, they would deliver neither son nor daughter; they would deliver but their own lives by their righteousness. (Ezek 14:13-20)

The questions that remains are, "If God's mercy expressed in his everlasting covenant is granted now to both Israel and the nations, does this mean that there is injustice or, at least, unfairness with God?" "Why was Israel given more than one chance whereas the nations are offered only the last one?" First and foremost, the message of the everlasting covenant is to the actual generation of its hearers in Israel who would thus be themselves receiving it for the first time. By the same token, when the nations hear the same message, they also hear of the stubborn disobedience of the previous generations of addressees. Therefore, for all intents and purposes, recipients of the message, both Jews and Gentiles, are on the same footing and there are de facto absolutely no privileges. Secondly, since the biblical narrative does not start with Jacob, but goes back to Abraham, Noah and Adam, and repeatedly includes the "sins" of the nations, then these nations are part of the narrative. Thirdly, and most importantly, the sinful experiences of the generations of the "forefathers" are an integral part of the heritage of the nations. Indeed, "you are a people holy to the Lord your God; the Lord your God has chosen you to be a people for his own possession,

out of all the peoples that are on the face of the earth" (Deut 7:6;
14:2), which means that Israel was one people or nation among
the rest of the peoples or nations. In Ezekiel, when it comes to
sinning, this close connection is expressed in a way that levels
any and all differences between Israel and the nations:

> Thus says the Lord God to Jerusalem: "Your origin and your birth
> are of the land of the Canaanites; your father was an Amorite, and
> your mother a Hittite ... You are the daughter of your mother,
> who loathed her husband and her children; and you are the sister
> of your sisters, who loathed their husbands and their children.
> Your mother was a Hittite and your father an Amorite. And your
> elder sister is Samaria, who lived with her daughters to the north
> of you; and your younger sister, who lived to the south of you, is
> Sodom with her daughters." (Ezek 16:1-3, 45-46)

This is precisely what allowed Paul to write authoritatively:

> I want you to know, brethren, that *our fathers* were all under the
> cloud, and all passed through the sea, and all were baptized into
> Moses in the cloud and in the sea, and all ate the same
> supernatural food and all drank the same supernatural drink. For
> they drank from the supernatural Rock which followed them, and
> the Rock was Christ. Nevertheless with most of them God was not
> pleased; for they were overthrown in the wilderness. *Now these*
> *things are warnings for us, not to desire evil as they did ... Now these*
> *things happened to them as a warning, but they were written down*
> *for our instruction, upon whom the end of the ages has come.* (1 Cor
> 10:1-6, 11)

The same Paul unequivocally stresses that God's final salvation
wrought through his Messiah indeed brought about a freedom
from exile and bondage, yet a freedom *under God's aegis* (Rom
6). Consequently, this freedom is secured for us so long as we
remain within the confines of God's will by abiding by "the law

of [his] Christ" (Gal 6:2), which is "the law of the Spirit of life" (Rom 8:2) heralded by Ezekiel. In Galatians the Apostle requires the fulfillment of the entire Law under the leadership of God's spirit:

> For you were called to freedom, brethren; only do not use your freedom as an opportunity for the flesh, but through love be servants of one another. For the whole law is fulfilled (*peplērōtai*) in one word, "You shall love your neighbor as yourself" ... But I say, walk (*peripateite*) by the Spirit, and do not fulfill (*telesēte*) the desire (*epithymian*) of the flesh. For the flesh desires (*epithymei*) against the Spirit, and the Spirit [is][20] against the flesh; for these are opposed to each other, to prevent you from *doing* what you would. But if you are led (*agesthe*) by the Spirit you are not under a law. Now the works of the flesh are plain ... I warn you, as I warned you before, that those who do (*prassontes*) such things shall not inherit the kingdom of God ... If we live by the Spirit, let us also walk (*stoikhōmen*) by the Spirit. (Gal 5:13-25)[21]

I kept close to the original text on purpose, in order to show how Paul was putting pressure on the Galatians not to do their own will, which is nothing other than the desire of the flesh (the human being). God granted them his spirit (3:2-5) in order for them to implement *his* will imbedded in his commandments. Should we not *do* so, then we shall have proven that we did not trust (have faith) indeed in his promise and consequently will not inherit his kingdom contained in this promise. The assuredness, then, is not a guarantee that we shall end up there,

---

[20] RSV has "the desires of the Spirit," which is quite against what Paul is saying. The spirit has a "will," not a "desire"; actually, under his guidance, "those who belong to Christ Jesus have crucified the flesh with its passions and desires" (v.24).

[21] I kept on purpose close to the original in order to underline the centrality of doing God's will. The verb *peripateō* (Greek), *halak* (halak), used in Gal 5:16, appears in the Old Testament in conjunction with the commands of the Law. The verb *stoikheō* is more forceful since it has the connotation of walking in line as in an army.

but stems from the guarantee that we have been turned back (returned)[22] to the right "way," which we shall have to "walk." The "way" in which we "stand (firm)" is still a "way" that we have to "walk":

> Therefore, since we are justified by trust (faith), we have (the eschatological) peace with God through our Lord Jesus Christ. Through him we have obtained *access* (*prosagōgēn*)[23] to this grace in which we *stand*, and we rejoice in our hope of sharing the glory of God. More than that, we rejoice in our sufferings, knowing that suffering produces endurance, and endurance produces character, and character produces hope, and *hope does not disappoint us*, because God's love has been poured into our hearts through the Holy Spirit which has been given to us. (Rom 5:1-5)

Thus a "believer" is someone who puts one's trust (*pistevōn*) in the *promise* of the Kingdom for which one has to hope *because* one has trusted, i.e., to hope *in that which* one has trusted. In the meantime, one is to express one's trust in God's (word of) promise by abiding by his (word of) commandments which are subsumed in the love for the others: "For through the Spirit, by faith, we wait for *the hope of righteousness.* For in Christ Jesus neither circumcision nor uncircumcision is of any avail, but faith working through love." (Gal 5:5-6) Hence, one is not *already* righteous in Christ; no issuance of any verdict is possible before God's final judgment. Rather, "righteousness by faith" means simply that one puts one's trust in God who has shown us and even put us on the "way" leading to his kingdom. This Point A, whereby we were returned from our wayward paths onto the right(eous) way, has been done through sheer gracefulness on

---

[22] See 1Thess 1:9; Gal 4:9.

[23] From the same root *ag*— as the verb *agesthe* (are led; Gal 5:18) with the preposition *pros* (toward).

God's part; we ourselves had no part in this action. Yet, although it is the way of life eternal, it is still a "way" that we have to walk in order to reach Point Z, life eternal. In order to reach that point we are to follow God's instruction given to us in the Law. Put otherwise, in order to walk that way, we have to walk in God's ways, which are not ours (Is; Ezek; Gal; Rom).

Consequently, faith is not, as it has unfortunately developed into, a formulaic expression of one's understanding of God's will or being, which one would pin down against the "faith" of others.[24] The original meaning of both the Hebrew 'aman and the Greek *pistevō* is to put one's trust in a statement *made by someone else and not by oneself.* This trust is expressed in an attitude. It is not a mental acquiescence to our own views. Otherwise, faithfulness is to ourselves and not to another. Now, when the required trust is in a word of promise, then we are to stay the course until the promise is realized. However, when that word of promise is linked to a covenant requiring that we follow certain rules, then our trust is expressed exclusively in our following those rules, and the only one who will judge if we are indeed doing so is the one who issued the covenant, and he will do so at the appointed time of judgment. This understanding is found at its clearest in Romans 1-2 and Mt 25: it is those who do God's will, *albeit unaware,* who will be found righteous, and not those who have a *mental* knowledge of it. Actually, the mental knowledge will play against those who "know":

And the Lord said: "Because this people draw near with their mouth and honor me with their lips, while their hearts are far from me, and their fear of me is a commandment of men learned by rote; therefore, behold, I will again do marvelous things with

---

[24] As, e.g., the "Orthodox faith" in contradistinction to the "Non-Chalcedonian," "Catholic," "Anglican," or "other like faiths."

this people, wonderful and marvelous; and the wisdom of their wise men shall perish, and the discernment of their discerning men shall be hid." (Is 29:13-14)

As for you, son of man, your people who talk together about you by the walls and at the doors of the houses, say to one another, each to his brother, "Come, and hear what the word is that comes forth from the Lord." And they come to you as people come, and they sit before you as my people, and they hear what you say but they will not do it; for with their lips they show much love, but their heart is set on their gain. And, lo, you are to them like one who sings love songs with a beautiful voice and plays well on an instrument, for they hear what you say, but they will not do it. (Ezek 31:30-32)

The Pauline epistles, then, are not so much "learning material" or even "teaching material" as a textbook would be, as they are "instructional" in the same sense as the *torah*. They assume Point A, which is that God, for no apparent reason, gave us access to the "way" leading unto salvation and life in his city, the Jerusalem above (Rom 5:1-11). That it is so for no apparent reason accounts for the central term "grace," an expression of God's inexplicable "delight": the Semitic phrase "to find grace in someone's eyes" means no more and no less than "to be liked by that someone," or "that someone likes us." This is the (humanly speaking) inexplicable premise with which the Pauline epistles start and end: "divine grace be with (to) you."[25] It is grace because the one who is delivering it is Paul the Apostle. A circumcised and Benjaminite son of Abraham, free in regards to any Jewish authority, and a Roman citizen, free in regards to the Gentiles he preached to, most of whom were slaves, he was commissioned as an headmaster (*oikonomos*) in the house of his

---

[25] Paul's best explanation in Rom 5:1-11 is that it cannot be explained!

master to be subservient to all (1 Cor 9:16-22). He actually is the tangible face of divine grace: his addressees can count their blessings that Paul was forcibly enlisted to carry the news of his message of salvation to the Gentiles by God who so has willed both to decide to save the Gentiles and to find a messenger to spread that news. And the way in which as well as the reason both actions were carried out are, as Second-Isaiah taught, not due to the worth or readiness of the recipients, but simply because it was God's sheer "delight, pleasurable will" (ḥapheṣ; Isaiah *passim*).[26] The following stop on the "way" after this initial Point A is the "peace" of the Kingdom, which is Point Z. Between these two there are no other points, there is just the "way" to be *followed and not chosen*, let alone mentally debated, by the recipients. This means that there is no upward progress on this road, as though one would "improve"—if so, then one would "earn" and not "inherit" the Kingdom!—but rather a forward movement not until the end of the road, but until the end "comes." The only "effort" on our part is to make sure that we be "on the road, on the way" (*en hodō*) when the end that is coming toward us arrives. Since we do not know "the time and the hour," this means that we are to stay (on) the course *at all times. Any slight deviation is catastrophic.* This, in turn, explains why Ezekiel and Second-Isaiah (Is 40-66), the prophets to Israel, relentlessly remind Israel of its forefathers' as well as its own sins: old habits may pop up again at any moment, and this time round there will be nothing other than ultimate (just) judgment, since ultimate mercy has been granted. This also explains why Paul, the Apostle to the nations, virtually never has words of praise, but rather expresses harshly his displeasure with his addressees.

---

[26] See Gen 34:19 where this verb means "to like." See also Num 14:8 where God delights in us on the condition that we follow his will.

Since Point A is already behind us all and Point Z is ahead of us all, Paul's letters cannot then be but exhortations to stay the course, paternal exhortations that are instructions to follow, in the same way as is the Torah (and the Prophets). Hence, the epistles are scripture inasmuch as they are written according to the scriptural fabric. They *are* scripture and do not need an outside authority to declare them so. Actually, Galatians, the first of and blueprint for any New Testament scripture, was written *against* any such authority. Yet, more importantly, since they are scripture, they are to be heard as such: straightforward instructions that need no explanation to be obeyed, and not as treatises or informational material about "theological" topics for the mental *passe-temps* of the believers. If they are not meant to bring us on a higher level of "knowledge"—"Knowledge puffs up, but love builds up" (1 Cor 8:1)—much less are they intended to bring us to an advanced level of self-righteous assuredness or a little further on our trek toward the Kingdom. There is actually no movement at all, and the hearers are thrown at the end of the letter back to the point at which they were at its beginning, a little beyond Point A which is behind them. Point Z, the eschatological peace, which is lumped "in hope" with Point A, God's graceful act of mercy, at the beginning of the letters (grace and peace be to you…), disappears at the end of the same letters leaving the hearers with only "grace be with you." This is precisely what Deuteronomy does, and I have shown that Galatians was actually conceived and written *à la* Deuteronomy.[27]

Most of us, who have been trained in theological discourse, often assume, without realizing it, that the biblical books are themselves theological discourses for us to use, to further

---

[27] *NTI₁* 35-6.

develop, or even to improve upon the thoughts imbedded in childish narratives for the commoner. But theological discourse is the product of the *human* mind. Scripture, on the other hand, repeatedly, if not relentlessly, presents itself as *divine* words coming from God's mind, which are inscribed *verbatim* by the sole recipient of these *words*. They are even delivered as such in a scroll whether the recipients hear them or not (Ezek 2-3); actually they are consigned in writing in a scroll *because* the recipients refused to hear them (Is 8:11-22 and Jer 36). And, if the scriptural assumption is that we, the hearers, refused, and keep refusing, to listen to the message, it does not make any sense for us to entertain the thought of analyzing that message to try to get information regarding our concerns, which may not even be the message's concerns. Accepting the message means to accept *its* concerns that are revealed within the message itself, and not brought into the message from outside. To plagiarize scripture itself, "the Lord's concerns are not (necessarily) our concerns, and his ways to go about them are not (necessarily) our ways" (Is 55:8). The real discrepancy actually lies in the "ways" to go about realities. Unfortunately, under the influence of philosophy and human discourse pervading the upper echelon of ecclesiastical leaders in the early centuries and their concern to dialogue philosophically with their non-Christian counterparts, theology developed into a discussion about God, man, salvation, life, death, eternal life, and the like, trying to give these ideas their "true definition or understanding." With time, such gave the false impression that scripture had a different, new, view of the meaning of words compared to their extant meaning. Ensued a differentiation between a physical realm and a spiritual one, a natural truth opposed to a theological-revelational one, a mystical reality beyond or deeper than a mere reality, and the like. One even began to speak of a Christian or theological versus a non-Christian or non-theological understanding of everyday realities such as man, life, death. Whereas, in reality, all the biblical terms were such common currency that everyone readily understood their meaning, and there was no need for further comments; otherwise, how would the hearers have been accountable for all the repeated indictments against them in the scriptural texts?

The proposed reading of Philippians in this commentary is actually a presentation of how the addressed hearers understood *immediately* the message of the Apostle that was read to them while gathered to hear it, without the luxury of being allowed to "take it home and study it," let alone discuss it. Instead of reading the epistle as though it were a philosophico-theological treatise to be dissected in order to "figure out" its deep(er) meaning in the "light" of a "theology" that developed later,[28] I shall endeavor to transpose my readers in time and space so that they become part of the Philippian gathering addressed by Paul. Once this is done, they will be able to *immediately* perceive Paul's message. Such an endeavor will simply entail an explanation of the terminology that was common currency for the Philippians but is not for us today. Nevertheless, this task is not as simple as it looks for the following reasons:

1. The Roman "world" is in many ways no more ours. The gods and the emperor, who were integral and essential parts of that world to the extent that it "rested" on them and their cult, are for us, for all practical purposes, non-entities. For us, their gods are simply not; they do not exist. At best, they are "demons," whereas for the Roman

---

[28] If anything, it is rather this later understanding that has to be not only explained but also *assessed* against the scriptural teaching.

Philippians they were "realities" of everyday life. For us, the cult of the emperor is a mere curiosity of the past and is even non-understandable, whereas for them it was the basis that held the empire together and thus all life within it.

2.   If our worldview is not theirs, then the meaning of the same words is not necessarily the same. And this is precisely our Achilles' heel when we deal with basic terms, such as power, salvation, gospel, faith, righteousness, peace, life, death, resurrection, heavens, earth. We assume that their meaning is obvious when, in fact, they reflect realities we are unfamiliar with. One can only begin to imagine the resulting mayhem when theologians start quoting scripture in support of their views. The worst aspect of this mayhem is that those who misuse scripture are often not even aware they are doing so.

Still the effort will prove to be worthwhile since it will allow my readers to engage firsthand with the text and make their own educated decisions regarding the meaning and intention of the scriptural book. In turn, such will broaden the constructive dialogue among those truly interested in submitting to the authority of scripture rather than using it as a tool for "guru-ism" in order to subjugate others and "glory in their flesh" (Gal 6:13), as the Apostle's opponents tired to do in Galatia. The Apostle was not interested in training the Galatians in "theological discourse" but in having them "inherit the kingdom of God" (Gal 5:21); similarly he was not interested in introducing the Philippians to "theology," but rather in having them "behave as citizens of the heavenly Jerusalem" (Phil 1:27; 3:20; see also Gal 4:26). Hopefully this present work will help my readers to join the community of the Apostle's Philippians while listening to his letter to them and thus be challenged not to "fathom" God's kingdom, but to inherit it.

In this commentary series, I have included both Greek and English texts for each verse. The English is the RSV translation, which I have been using in my writings. In my comments, however, I often defer to the Greek with my own translation in order to render the meaning as close as possible to the original text.

Chapter 1

Vv. 1-2 ¹Παῦλος καὶ Τιμόθεος δοῦλοι Χριστοῦ Ἰησοῦ πᾶσιν τοῖς ἁγίοις ἐν Χριστῷ Ἰησοῦ τοῖς οὖσιν ἐν Φιλίπποις σὺν ἐπισκόποις καὶ διακόνοις, ²χάρις ὑμῖν καὶ εἰρήνη ἀπὸ θεοῦ πατρὸς ἡμῶν καὶ κυρίου Ἰησοῦ Χριστοῦ.

¹Paul and Timothy, servants of Christ Jesus, to all the saints in Christ Jesus who are at Philippi, with the bishops and deacons: ²Grace to you and peace from God our Father and the Lord Jesus Christ.

As usual, the introductory salutation functions also as a compendium of the letter content itself. This is understandable: before writing, the author already knows what he is about to say and this knowledge influences the terminology he chooses in his salutation. There are two specific characteristics of our letter's introduction, especially when compared to those of the other epistles: the epithet "slaves" (servants) associated with the senders and the special reference to "bishops and deacons" among the addressees. A more detailed study of these two features will readily show that they were dictated by the letter's intent.

Only here is Timothy introduced both on a par with Paul and with the same title. In 1 Corinthians and Colossians, Paul is an apostle while Timothy is just a brother; the same differentiation is found in Philemon where only Paul is a (chained) prisoner compared to the brother Timothy. In 1 and 2 Thessalonians, Timothy is on a par with Paul; however neither has a title and Timothy comes in third position after Silvanus.[1] In Philippians,

---

[1] See more on Silvanus in my *NTI₄* 95-96.

we encounter Timothy in a position of authority equal to Paul's, yet this authority is, as it were, "from below," linked to the status of slavery as it is in Philemon. In the latter, to make his plea on behalf of the slave Onesimus more pertinent, the Apostle presents himself in a similar position of someone who is not free. To drive home the point even more, Paul refers to himself repeatedly as a (chained) prisoner: vv.1 and 9. In v.9 he even stresses the fact that he was actually demoted to this position while being in God's service: "yet for love's sake I prefer to appeal to you, I, Paul, an ambassador and now a prisoner also for Christ Jesus." In Philippians, thrust in the garb of a testament, Paul's intention is to imprint upon all "servitude to God" as the legacy to be maintained throughout one's life.[2] To do so, he first introduces not only himself, but also Timothy, his heir apparent (2:19-24), as a "slave of the Christ Jesus." Thus servitude is indeed a legacy to be maintained, and not only Paul's fateful personal experience. On the other hand, if it applies to Timothy, Paul's heir, then it applies all the more to "all the saints" in Philippi since their status as saints is no different than that of Paul and Timothy: it was and is secured through the Christ Jesus whose slaves the latter are. Furthermore, if this legacy includes Timothy as plenipotentiary leader of all the Gentile churches after Paul, then it is not only the common Philippian believers that are bound by it, but also their leaders, the "bishops and deacons." This is precisely the intention behind including the latter in the salutation, a unique case in Pauline literature.

This approach of belittling, to the lowest possible degree, the leaders of a community before and to the hearing of their followers is unconventional, to say the least. After all, one is free to present oneself modestly, but what Paul is doing here is a far

---

[2] He does the same in ch.6 of Romans.

cry from educational self-abasement. He is officially imposing upon Timothy and the bishops and deacons to be and thus act as "slaves" to their juniors as Paul himself does (1 Cor 9:19-23). Later in the letter, it becomes clear why he feels entitled to do this. When inviting, in turn, all the believers, and especially the leaders among them,[3] to humility (2:3) and obedience (v.12), he does so by asking them to follow in the footsteps of Christ himself whom he depicts as having humbled himself as an obedient slave (vv.7-8). It is then the example of Christ that Paul himself is following. That is why, throughout the letter, whenever he offers himself as an example (1:29-30; 3:17; 4:9), he is actually understanding it in the manner of his request to the Corinthians and the Thessalonians: "Be imitators of me, as I am of Christ" (1 Cor 11:1); "And you became imitators of us and of the Lord." (1 Thess 1:6)

For Paul, anyone who has accepted the terms of his gospel, which is the eschatological "law" (*torah-nomos*; Rom 8:2; Gal 6:2) of the eschatological covenant (2 Cor 3:6) spoken of in Jeremiah and Ezekiel (Jer 31:31-34: Ezek 11:19; 34:25; 36:26; 37:26) and supposed to reach the nations (Is 42:1-7; 49:1-6), is bound to be a "slave unto others" (Gal 5:13). On the other hand, the divine law is actually what sets God's people apart, making them "holy" (separated), just as God himself is "holy."[4] This is actually what ultimately differentiates Jew from Gentile: "Then what advantage has the Jew? Or what is the value of circumcision? Much in every way. To begin with, the Jews are entrusted with the oracles of God." (Rom 3:1-2) However, the Law is a set of commandments by which one is to abide, and is not "correct formulas of belief." Consequently, to be a saint is

---

[3] See my comments below on 2:1-4.
[4] The original meaning of holiness is taboo.

equivalent to having been called unto sanctification, unto behaving as a saint must: "To all God's beloved in Rome, who are called to be saints" (Rom 1:7); "To the church of God which is at Corinth, to those sanctified in Christ Jesus, called to be saints" (1 Cor 1:2); "For God has not called us for uncleanness, but in(to) holiness." (1 Thess 4:7) That is why one cannot be a saint nominally:

> Do you not know that the unrighteous will not inherit the kingdom of God? Do not be deceived; neither the immoral, nor idolaters, nor adulterers, nor sexual perverts, nor thieves, nor the greedy, nor drunkards, nor revilers, nor robbers will inherit the kingdom of God. And such were some of you. But you were washed, you were sanctified, you were justified in the name of the Lord Jesus Christ and in the Spirit of our God. (1 Cor 6:9-11)

If the saints are the members of the messianic community, then they are to abide by the Messiah's law (Gal 6:2). Since Paul and Timothy are the primary and thus referential members of any messianic community, at least where the church in Philippi is concerned, then pressure is put on the Philippians early on: to be a saint is equivalent to being an obedient slave in God's household, doing his will. The practical conclusion—full and unequivocal submission to God's will—comes later when Christ himself, who is introduced here as "lord" (Phil 1:2), will be given as the ultimate example of the obedient slave: "Therefore, my beloved, as you have always obeyed, so now, not only as in my presence but much more in my absence, work out your own salvation with fear and trembling; *for God is at work in you, both to will and to work for his good pleasure.*" (2:12-13)

Who or what are the bishops and deacons? First and foremost, one should not, as is often done, read later developments back into these appellations. Such would require from us extra care since these two terms are very important in the ecclesiastical terminology of the traditional churches. Let me begin with "deacon" (*diakonos*) since it is much more common than "bishop" in the New Testament; furthermore, Paul uses it of himself and his colleagues, which might help our investigation. It is clear from the many instances of the root *diakon—* in the New Testament that it refers to service a lesser human being offers or gives to someone of higher rank, and thus is practically equivalent in meaning to the root *doul—* whence is *doulos* (slave). Can we be more specific as to the difference or, at least nuance, between the two?

A good starting point is the instances where the root *diakon—* occurs in a setting that is not necessarily specifically related to church life. The most "neutral" instance is found in Luke 17:8 as part of Jesus' teaching, that is to say, not referring to someone in particular:

> Will any one of you, who has a servant (*doulon*) plowing or keeping sheep, say to him when he has come in from the field, 'Come at once and sit down at table'? Will he not rather say to him, 'Prepare supper for me, and gird yourself and serve (*diakonei*) me, till I eat and drink; and afterward you shall eat and drink'? Does he thank the servant (*doulō*) because he did what was commanded? (Lk 17:7-9)

The conclusion is inescapable. Given that the *diakonia* here occurs as a verb qualifying the service that a slave does, it is clear that a deacon is none other than a slave *while he is waiting at tables*. Put otherwise, slavery is a state or status; diaconate is functional: a slave is always a slave, while a deacon is not always a deacon. This conclusion is corroborated in a Johannine passage where we find the same general terminology in conjunction with table fellowship as in the Lukan passage just cited: "Six days before the Passover, Jesus came to Bethany, where Lazarus was, whom Jesus had raised from the dead. There they made him a supper; Martha was serving (*diēkonei*), and Lazarus was one of those at table with him." (Jn 12:1-2)[5]

This understanding of *diakonia* can be seen in the pericope in Acts where we read about the official institution of the "diaconate" in church life:

> Now in these days when the disciples were increasing in number, the Hellenists murmured against the Hebrews because their widows were neglected in the daily distribution (*diakonia*). And the twelve summoned the body of the disciples and said, "It is not right that we should give up preaching the word of God to serve (*diakonein*) tables. Therefore, brethren, pick out from among you seven men of good repute, full of the Spirit and of wisdom, whom we may appoint to this duty. But we will devote ourselves to prayer and to the ministry (*diakonia*) of the word." (6:1-4).

One finds here a clear instance of the classic weakness of translations in general. The same word *diakonia* is translated differently, giving the impression that the handling of the (gospel) word is of a different nature than that of the daily bread. Even more: it is actually the noun *diakonia*, which is specifically a table fellowship term, that actually defines and qualifies the so-

---

[5] The same applies to the following Lukan passage, parallel to ours, where the justified assumption is that Martha invited Jesus into her house and served him something to eat (which is dutiful in the Middle East): "Now as they went on their way, he entered a village; and a woman named Martha received him (into her house). And she had a sister called Mary, who sat at the Lord's feet and listened to his teaching. But Martha was distracted with much serving (*diakonian*); and she went to him and said, 'Lord, do you not care that my sister has left me to serve (*diakonein*) alone? Tell her then to help me.'" (Lk 10:38-40)

called "ministry" of the word. Put otherwise, the ministry is to be understood against the metaphor of feeding, and not vice versa. Consequently, in order for the divine word to be indeed food for every man (Deut 8:3) it has to be administered at a table gathering. This is precisely what we find stressed repeatedly in Acts. Notice how the meal is the matrix of the following passage:

> On the first day of the week, when we were gathered together to break bread, Paul talked with them, intending to depart on the morrow; and he prolonged his speech until midnight. There were many lights in the upper chamber where we were gathered. And a young man named Eutychus was sitting in the window. He sank into a deep sleep as Paul talked still longer; and being overcome by sleep, he fell down from the third story and was taken up dead. But Paul went down and bent over him, and embracing him said, "Do not be alarmed, for his life is in him." And when Paul had gone up and had broken bread and eaten, he conversed with them a long while, until daybreak, and so departed. And they took the lad away alive, and were not a little comforted. (27:7-12)

The death and the raising of the young man are totally downplayed and do not interrupt Paul's teaching *while breaking bread* with his listeners. The centrality of the teaching at table fellowship is found in the Lukan paradigmatic compendium describing the life of the community around the apostolic word:

> So those who received his [Peter's] word were baptized, and there were added that day about three thousand souls. And they devoted themselves to the apostles' teaching and fellowship (*koinōnia*), to the breaking of bread and the prayer. And fear came upon every soul; and many wonders and signs were done through the apostles. And all who believed were together (*epi to avto*) and had all things in common (*koina*); and they sold their possessions and goods and distributed them to all, as any had need. And day by day, attending the temple together and breaking bread *in their homes*,

they partook of food with glad and generous hearts praising God
and having favor with all the people. And the Lord added to their
number those who were being saved day by day *together* with them
(*epi to avto*).[6] (Acts 2:41-47)

This centrality, if not essentiality, of table fellowship is also
found in Paul's statement: "The cup of blessing which we bless,
is it not a participation (*koinōnia*) in the blood of Christ? The
bread which we break, is it not a participation (*koinōnia*) in the
body of Christ? Because there is one bread, we who are many are
one body, for we all partake of the one bread." (1 Cor 10:16-17)
What is clearly stressed in the reality of fellowship is the oneness,
obviously in the sense of being "at one." However, this oneness is
not an intellectual reality, as in saying the same creed formula;
rather it is a practical oneness expressed in the oneness of the
table. This is made clear later in the epistle where Paul threatens
the Corinthians with God's ultimate wrath if they do not eat
together, the reason being that the oneness of the table hangs on
the oneness of the Lord (11:17-34). Thus, duality of tables is not
allowed.

 All the preceding clearly points back to Galatians 2:1-14,
which is the axial passage around which are woven the teachings
as well as the narratives of the entire New Testament.[7] There we
find precisely that the real test for the fellowship (*koinōnia*)
between the Jerusalem pillars, on the one hand, and Paul and
Barnabas, on the other hand (Gal 2:9), is not another debate of
words and wordings, but the actuality of the one table (vv.11-
14). It is this kind of crisis at Antioch that precipitated the break
between not only Paul and Peter, but even between Paul and his

---

[6] RSV omits the translation of the last phrase *epi to avto*, which it translated as
"together" earlier in v. 44.
[7] See my 4 volumes of *New Testament Introduction: NTI₁, NTI₂, NTI₃, NTI₄*.

co-apostle Barnabas who was on his side when the hand-shake of
the *koinōnia* was sealed!

Yet, here again, as in the case of "bishops and deacons," the
greatest danger lies in reading back one's practice and
understanding of our contemporary Eucharistic gathering into
New Testament times. The Lukan paradigmatic compendium
quoted above (Acts 2:41-47) clearly and unequivocally states that
the breaking of bread took place "in their homes," indicating
that it was a regular meal and not some sort of a "religious" meal
at a "religious" place. Notice the actual differentiation in Luke's
wording between two such gatherings: "And day by day,
attending the temple together and breaking bread in their homes
(*kat' oikon*; at home)." (v.46) This is only understandable if one
recalls that the emerging Pauline "communities" were not yet
part of a *religio licita*. Consequently, these home gatherings were
not just *ad hoc* informal meals, but factually the actual Pauline
"churches" as is clear from the following instances: "Greet Prisca
and Aquila, my fellow workers in Christ Jesus ... greet also the
church in their house" (Rom 16:3, 5); "The churches of Asia
send greetings. Aquila and Prisca, together with the church in
their house, send you hearty greetings in the Lord" (1 Cor
16:19); "Give my greetings to the brethren at Laodicea, and to
Nympha and the church in her house" (Col 4:15); "To
Philemon our beloved fellow worker ... and the church in your
house." (Philem 1-2)[8]

Two conclusions are in order. The first is that Paul's frequent
use of the root *diakon*— together with that of *doul*— to refer to
himself and his co-workers in conjunction with their apostolic

---

[8] See also Paul's words to the elders of Ephesus: "I did not shrink from declaring to
you anything that was profitable, and teaching you in public and from house to
house." (Acts 20:20)

activity[9] was not fanciful on his part, but rather intended. His apostleship, as he wrote in Galatians 2, was continually tested at table fellowship whereby Jews and Gentiles were to be de facto "at one" by sharing the "one" table. The second conclusion is that the diaconate, which is the service of tables without differentiation between Jews and Gentiles or Hebrews and Hellenists (Acts 6:1-5), was an integral part of the church gatherings.

Given that Paul's letter was addressed to be read at a church gathering, can our conclusion concerning the deacons be of help in determining what bishops were all about? I believe it can and it does. One can start by surmising that their function is to secure the other facet of the gathering, the "ministry (*diakonia*) of the word" (Acts 6:4). A look at the New Testament will readily confirm this conclusion. The Greek *episkopos* means "overseer," someone who looks over with the intention of taking care of someone or something else. Although the verb *episkopein* (Heb 12:14) has the same meaning as its plain cognate *skopein* (see to it; pay attention to; be careful to; as in Lk 11:35; Rom 16:17; 2 Cor 4:18; Gal 6:1; Phil 2:14; 3:17), the noun *episkopos* reflects the responsibility of a leader for those who are in his care, as is clear from Acts 20:28: "Take heed to yourselves and to all the flock, in which the Holy Spirit has made you overseers (*episkopous*), to care for the church of God which he obtained with the blood of his own Son." This passage sheds light on the plural "bishops" in Philippians since the addressees in Acts are none other than the "elders" of Ephesus (Acts 20:17). However, what is more interesting for our case is the link made here between overseeing and shepherding, which is also found in 1

---

[9] Rom 11:13; 15:31; 1 Cor 3:5; 2 Cor 3:3-9; 4:1; 5:18; 6:3, 4; 11:8, 15, 23; Gal 2:17; Eph 3:7; 4:11-12; 6:21; Col 1:7, 23, 25; 4:7; 1 Tim 1:12; 2 Tim 4:5, 11.

Peter 2:5 to speak of God himself: "For you were straying like sheep, but have now returned to the Shepherd and Guardian (*episkopon*) of your souls."[10] On the other hand, *episkopē*, which refers to the activity itself of overseeing, is used to speak of the apostolic office in Acts 1:20. The three remaining occurrences of this noun speak of either the office of bishop (overseer; 1 Tim 3:1) or of divine visitation for judgment as an "overseer" would do (Lk 19:44; 1 Pet 2:12). The only possible bridge among all these seemingly disjointed connotations is the original Hebrew *paqad* that reflects the visitation of an overseer, a senior who "looks after." However, this visit can be with either the positive intent of taking care in mercy or the negative intent of judging and condemning.[11] These two facets are intertwined in Ezekiel 34 where God, in his visitation, is the shepherd who brings salvation to his sheep and harshly punishes those whom he had assigned as shepherds over them. And he does so at the same time through the prophetic word, which is both for instruction and, if not heeded, for judgment.

The overseer then is the New Testament "prophet" who continues the apostolic activity of preaching and teaching the divine word, while the deacon continues the apostolic activity of securing the oneness of the table. This understanding of the bishop as "prophet" is supported by the fact that the plural "bishops" (Phil 1:1) corresponds to the plurality of "prophets" in the one church gathering (1 Cor 14). One finds further corroboration in the Pastoral Epistles whose intent is to ensure the continuation of the apostolic activity after the Apostle's

---

[10] This explains the addition *episkopountes* in 1 Pet 5:2, which is found in a few manuscripts: "Tend the flock of God that is your charge, [looking (*episkopountes*)] not by constraint but willingly, not for shameful gain but eagerly..."

[11] Hence the same *episkopein* and *episkopē* translate also the Hebrew *daraš* (study, examine; e.g. Deut 11:12).

death. Just as the prophet is second to the apostle (1 Cor 12:28), so are Timothy and Titus who, as bishops, are entrusted with a "deposit" that the apostle alone carries as the (living) "tradition" until it is laid down in an unchangeable written form (the deposit) for the ages. Furthermore, bishops are to heed and uphold the scriptural word in the same manner as was required from the elders-bishops of Ephesus, whose elder-bishop is now Timothy: "Take heed to yourself and to your teaching; hold to that, for by so doing you will save both yourself and your hearers." (1 Tim 4:16)[12] That bishops are bound by the apostolic teaching in both of its features, the teaching and the *diakonia*, is best seen in another "testament" of Paul's:

> I charge you in the presence of God and of Christ Jesus who is to judge the living and the dead, and by his appearing and his kingdom: preach the word, be urgent in season and out of season, convince, rebuke, and exhort, be unfailing in patience and in teaching. For the time is coming when people will not endure sound teaching, but having itching ears they will accumulate for themselves teachers to suit their own likings, and will turn away from listening to the truth and wander into myths. As for you, always be steady, endure suffering, do the work of an evangelist, fulfill your ministry (*diakonian*). (2 Tim 4:1-5)

This trajectory culminates in the epistle that epitomizes the Pauline teaching and is addressed to the church of Ephesus, where the gifts of which 1 Corinthians speak boil down to the following list: "And his gifts were that some should be apostles, some prophets, some evangelists, some pastors and teachers." (Eph 4:11). Not only is the list brought down to the three primary gifts which are related to the communication of the

---

[12] Compare with the text quoted earlier: "Take heed to yourselves and to all the *flock*, in which the Holy Spirit has made you overseers." (Acts 20:28)

word (apostles, prophets, teachers), but it also expands the gift of prophecy in 1 Corinthians to include "evangelists and pastors (shepherds)." The first, evangelist, is used of Timothy in the above quoted passage (2 Tim 4:5)[13] and the second, shepherds (*poimenas*), has been discussed at length earlier. And here once more, Paul's specter looms high in the background: already in his apologia and thus delineation of apostleship in 1 Corinthians 9, we have the seed of the view that the apostle, and thus every evangelist (carrier of the gospel teaching), is likened to a shepherd: "Who tends (*poimainei*) a flock (*poimnēn*) without getting some of the milk (of the flock; *tēs poimnēs*)?" (v.7)

In this magisterially worded salutation, the author of this Pauline testament to the church in Philippi succeeded in establishing the path that should be followed in the Pauline churches at the Apostle's death and until he comes back with the Lord: (1) Timothy is his heir; (2) the gatherings are to be around the apostolic word expounded by bishops at the occasion of every common meal on the condition that deacons ensure the "oneness of the table"; (3) until the Lord's coming all are bound to be, as Paul is and Timothy has no choice but to be, "slaves" in God's household, obedient to his will exclusively; (4) God's will boils down to utter humility toward one another after the example set by God's plenipotentiary emissary, the messiah, whose perfect image the Philippians have in "Paul in chains."

This path is indeed a "way" that is defined by the biblical narrative since the word of God that Paul preached is nothing other than God's word that is embedded once and for all in scripture: "Paul, a servant of Jesus Christ, called to be an apostle,

---

[13] The only other instance in the New Testament is "Philip the evangelist" (Acts 21:8) in honor of his having been the first who preached the gospel to the nations (Acts 8).

set apart for the gospel of God which he promised beforehand through his prophets in the holy scriptures." (Rom 1:1-2) Our acceptance of this word integrates us into the biblical narrative, as Paul taught the Gentile Corinthians:

> I want you to know, brethren, that our fathers were all under the cloud, and all passed through the sea, and all were baptized into Moses in the cloud and in the sea, and all ate the same supernatural food and all drank the same supernatural drink. For they drank from the supernatural Rock which followed them, and the Rock was Christ. Nevertheless with most of them God was not pleased; for they were overthrown in the wilderness. Now these things are warnings for us, not to desire evil as they did … Now these things happened to them as a warning, but they were written down for our instruction, upon whom the end of the ages has come. (1 Cor 10:1-6, 11)

Our acceptance of God's word puts us on the "way" that was and is offered to the biblical Israel and, through God's chosen one, to the nations (Is 42:1-7; 49:1-6). The beginning of that "way" is already behind us; it took place when we were lost, scattered, enslaved, in darkness, and God, for no apparent reason, "called" us out of our misery and set us "on the way" toward "a land of milk and honey" where we would find life and safety.

To do good to someone for no apparent reason—especially when the situation of distress is of one's own doing—is an act of "grace" (*kharis*). This term is the translation of the Hebrew *ḥen* encountered in the expression "to find *ḥen* in someone's eyes," meaning "to be liked by someone," "someone likes (us)." The connotation is that the entire matter is out of our hands. We are merely the recipients of such, should our decision be to accept it. However, the initial offer is entirely bound to the one who makes the offer. In the case of the Philippians, God's offer to them was made through Paul. The mere fact that the latter calls them "saints" means that they are already "on the way" and thus that the act of grace is behind them.

Paul's greeting, however, adds the wish of peace (*eirēnē*). This is the Hebrew *šalom* whose basic meaning is the state of being *šalem* (sane, healthy, as someone or something is supposed to be). It is not a super-state in any way, just the state of how matters are supposed to be. However, in scripture, matters are the way they are supposed to be only when they are according to God's will. Hence, this state of "peace" is actually dismantled when we do not abide by the precepts of God that are our guide "on the way" on which God has put us. Contravening the divine precepts as communicated by God through his prophets and then lain down in scripture is the reason why there is "no peace." This understanding of peace explains the Pauline vocabulary whereby sinners are God's "enemies" (*ekhthroi*) and their status is one of "enmity" (*ekhthra*).[14] The simplest way to view the entire matter is through the story of Adam in Genesis 2-3. He was "in (God's) peace" or "at peace (with God)" so long as he did not contravene God's express command (Gen 2:16-17). The moment he did, the divine curse struck and he lost the garden that God had planted for him to enjoy (2:8; 3:23-24). Later, the same will occur to Israel when the people are driven out of the earth granted to them. Although this "peace" is lost, God intervenes with his "grace" and offers the people the opportunity to "turn back" (*šub*) to the "way" (*derek*) that would eventually make them "return" (*šub*) to God's "(place of) peace."

---

[14] Rom 5:10; 8:7; 11:28; Eph 2:14, 16; Col 1:21.

Thus, there is a difference between the wish of grace and that of peace in Paul's greetings. The first is actually a reminder of the grace that was already granted. The second, however, is a reminder of what lies ahead; it is wished "on the hope" that the Philippians would attain it, should they abide by the Apostle's instructions as laid down in his epistle. This explains why, at the end of the letter, Paul takes leave from them by wishing them only "grace" (4:23). The "peace," he cannot guarantee as he does "grace" since the former is conditioned on whether they will have abided by his precepts, which is a matter obviously out of his hands.

Both this grace (and the way it opened) and peace are granted by God, who has become the father of the Philippians by making them, though Gentiles, members of his household: "So then you are no longer strangers and sojourners, but you are fellow citizens with the saints and members of the household (*oikoioi*) of God" (Eph 2:19); "So then, as we have opportunity, let us do good to all men, and especially to those who are members of the household (*oikoious*) of faith." (Gal 6:10) God implemented his will over his household through his obedient servant, the Christ Jesus, as Paul will explain in Philippians 2:6-11. This servant's total and trusting obedience made the head of the household fully trust him and assign him as "lord" over his household, just as a chief steward (*oikonomos*) would be (Lk 12:42).[15] In this sense divine grace and peace are granted by God the Father primarily (Col 1:2) and also by the Lord Jesus Christ, the relationship between their authorities being similar to that of

---

[15] "Who then is the faithful and wise steward (*oikonomos*), whom his master will set over his household, to give them their portion of food at the proper time?" See also 1 Cor 4:1-2: "This is how one should regard us, as servants of Christ and stewards (*oikonomous*) of the mysteries of God. Moreover it is required of stewards that they be found trustworthy."

Pharaoh and Joseph (Gen 41:37-45): just as Pharaoh granted full authority to Joseph, God did so with his Christ Jesus (Phil 2:9-11).

Vv. 3-7 ³Εὐχαριστῶ τῷ θεῷ μου ἐπὶ πάσῃ τῇ μνείᾳ ὑμῶν ⁴πάντοτε ἐν πάσῃ δεήσει μου ὑπὲρ πάντων ὑμῶν, μετὰ χαρᾶς τὴν δέησιν ποιούμενος, ⁵ἐπὶ τῇ κοινωνίᾳ ὑμῶν εἰς τὸ εὐαγγέλιον ἀπὸ τῆς πρώτης ἡμέρας ἄχρι τοῦ νῦν, ⁶πεποιθὼς αὐτὸ τοῦτο, ὅτι ὁ ἐναρξάμενος ἐν ὑμῖν ἔργον ἀγαθὸν ἐπιτελέσει ἄχρι ἡμέρας Χριστοῦ Ἰησοῦ· ⁷ Καθώς ἐστιν δίκαιον ἐμοὶ τοῦτο φρονεῖν ὑπὲρ πάντων ὑμῶν διὰ τὸ ἔχειν με ἐν τῇ καρδίᾳ ὑμᾶς, ἔν τε τοῖς δεσμοῖς μου καὶ ἐν τῇ ἀπολογίᾳ καὶ βεβαιώσει τοῦ εὐαγγελίου συγκοινωνούς μου τῆς χάριτος πάντας ὑμᾶς ὄντας.

> ³*I thank my God in all my remembrance of you,* ⁴*always in every prayer of mine for you all making my prayer with joy,* ⁵*thankful for your partnership in the gospel from the first day until now.* ⁶*And I am sure that he who began a good work in you will bring it to completion at the day of Jesus Christ.* ⁷*It is right for me to feel thus about you all, because I hold you in my heart, for you are all partakers with me of grace, both in my imprisonment and in the defense and confirmation of the gospel.*

Since everything (grace and the promised peace) for the Philippians started with Paul, he begins by recalling their story together. He himself, most probably, is about to finish the course, while they are still on it. He prays for all of them all the time, as only a high priest would, and that he is indeed. This is how he views himself in Romans: "But on some points I have written to you very boldly by way of reminder, because of the grace given me by God to be a minister (*leitourgon*; "liturg," celebrant of a liturgy) of Christ Jesus to the Gentiles in the priestly service (*hierourgounta*; "hierourgizing," performing a priestly function) of the gospel of God, so that the offering (*prosphora*) of the Gentiles may be acceptable, sanctified by the Holy Spirit." (15:15-16) He will use a similar terminology later in this epistle: "Even if I am to be poured as a libation (*spendomai*) upon the sacrificial (*thysia*; sacrifice) offering (*leitourgia*; liturgy, temple service) of your faith,[16] I am glad and rejoice with you all." (Phil 2:17) This statement is closely linked to the prayer of thanksgiving (1:3-4) in that both are done with joy.[17] In 2 Timothy, his other testament, we encounter the only other instance of *spendomai* in conjunction with Paul's last stretch on the "way":

> For I am already on the point of being sacrificed (as a libation; *spendomai*); the time of my departure has come. I have fought the good fight, I have finished the race, I have kept the faith. Henceforth there is laid up for me the crown of righteousness, which the Lord, the righteous judge, will award to me on that Day, and not only to me but also to all who have loved his appearing. (4:6-8)

Consequently, in his thanksgiving prayer (Phil 1:3-4) Paul is laying the groundwork for what he will develop later in the epistle: asking the Philippians to follow his example and stay the course as he did and is now about to finish.

As for the joy (*khara; simḥah*) with which Paul lifts up his prayer to God, it has to do with the fact that joy in scripture is eschatological in that it is linked with the heavenly Jerusalem and its peace.[18] Moreover, since this joy, though "coming," is

---

[16] The Greek reads *epi tē thysia kai leitourgia tēs pisteōs hymōn* "upon the (bloody) sacrifice and liturgy of your faith."

[17] See below on the importance of joy as an essential ingredient in Paul's high-priestly prayer.

[18] See my *OTI₃* 30-32.

nevertheless assured inasmuch as the gospel is a word of assurance (1:6) it is to be felt within and in spite of the afflictions in this world: "What then? Only that in every way, whether in pretense or in truth, Christ is proclaimed; and in that I rejoice. Yes, and I shall rejoice" (1:18-19); "And you became imitators of us and of the Lord, for you received the word in much affliction, with joy inspired by the Holy Spirit." (1 Thess 1:6) Actually, for Paul, affliction, as much as joy, is an integral part of the gospel message: "For when we were with you, we told you beforehand that we were to suffer affliction; just as it has come to pass, and as you know." (1 Thess 3:4) That is why Paul, later in Philippians, will use the same expression *synkoinōnia* (communion with ; partaking with) to speak of affliction as he does when referring to the grace (free gift) bestowed by God: "It is right for me to feel thus about you all, because I hold you in my heart, for you are all partakers (*synkoinōnous*) with me of grace, both in my imprisonment and in the defense and confirmation of the gospel" (Phil 1:7); "Yet it was kind of you to share (*synkoinōnēsantes*) my trouble (*thlipsei*; affliction)." (4:14)

This reality of the close link between joy and affliction is grounded in that the actual *koinōnia* (partnership; fellowship; sharing) between the Apostle and the Philippians is "in the gospel" he preached to them, which is precisely the essential reason for his prayer of thanksgiving: "(thankful) for your partnership (*koinōnia*) in the gospel from the first day until now." (1:5) This term was discussed earlier in conjunction with "bishops and deacons," and it was showed that its basic connotation is table fellowship during which, instead of entertaining chatter, the scriptural word was shared (made common, *koinos*). As I explained above, the entire Pauline teaching in all his letters is anchored in and revolves around what he said in his earliest epistle (Gal 2:1-14). In Philippians, we find this confirmed in that Paul's basic request of his apparent heir is the oneness (of table fellowship) between Jews and Gentiles: "I entreat Euodia and I entreat Syntyche to agree in the Lord." (4:2)[19]

As usual and as already discussed above, the epistle's introduction is a compendium of its entirety. This general rule is at its clearest in the one sentence (in Greek) prayerful introduction (1:3-7). The Philippians' special place among all his communities will be explained later in chapter 4. Geographically, Philippi is the city in which Paul preached the gospel for the first time outside the boundaries of Judaism. He may have done this for a reason. Philippi was at the same time (1) in the land of Alexander who was the first to spread Hellenism (and thus the Gentile way par excellence) widely beyond the borders of classical Greece; (2) renamed after Alexander's father, Philip II, who united Macedonia and conquered Illyria, Thrace, and Greece; (3) a Roman colony starting in 42 B.C. and thus a mini-Rome; (4) situated on the *Via Egnatia* that linked Asia Minor to Italy. So from "the first day" the gospel, which is nothing other than the *torah* preached to the nations, was linked to the name of Philippi, as Paul will clearly spell out later: "And you Philippians yourselves know that *in the beginning of the gospel, when I left Macedonia*, no church entered into partnership (*ekoinōnēsen*) with me in giving and receiving except you only." (4:15) If the "beginning of the gospel" is linked to Paul's leaving Macedonia rather than entering it, this means that actually the gospel was "born" *in* Macedonia when its message was accepted by a few Gentiles who joined in table fellowship with the Jew Paul and his Jewish colleagues. The gospel seed that faltered in Antioch in

---

[19] See my comments below on this verse.

the "land" of Judaism bore fruit in the "land" of Philip and Alexander.

The Philippians have maintained the partnership in the gospel until now. Yet, Paul does not thank them for that. Rather, thanksgiving is due solely to God since he is the one who "began the good work of the gospel"[20] among the Philippians, who will, Paul is "sure" (*pepoithōs*; confident), ensure that the good work will be brought to full fruition *until* the day of Christ Jesus.[21] If God can do that, then he is definitely the one who has maintained that good work *until* now (the time of the epistle writing), and thanksgiving is due to him at all times (*pantote*; always, 1:4). It is actually well that God is all along in control; otherwise the Philippians may risk ending up not "pure and blameless on that day of Christ" (v.10), which is the day of the final judgment: "… on that day when, according to my gospel, God judges the secrets of men by Christ Jesus." (Rom 2:16)

The mention of judgment day allows Paul to ease into preparing the Philippians for his eventual—actually very probable—death, which will leave them bereft of him until either that day or their own end. At any rate, he wants to console them by pointing out that his end is not *the* end. To do so, he writes that their partnership in the gospel of grace (Phil 1:5)

---

[20] Notice the close terminological parallelism between Phil 1:5-6 (thankful for your partnership [*koinōnia*] in the gospel from the first day until now. And I am sure that he who began [*enarxamenos*] a good work in you will bring it to completion at the day of Jesus Christ) and 4:15 (And you Philippians yourselves know that in the beginning [*arkhē*] of the gospel, when I left Macedonia, no church entered into partnership (*ekoinōnēsen*) with me in giving and receiving except you only). *enarxamenos* and *arkhē* are from the same root.

[21] The couple *enarkhomai* (begin) and *epiteleō* (fulfill; bring to completion; complete) is also found in Gal 3:3 where Paul uses it disparagingly against the Galatians whom he mocks for working in the opposite direction than God: "Are you so foolish? Having begun (*enarxamenoi*) with the Spirit, are you now ending (*epiteleisthe*) with the flesh?"

means partnership in all that that grace entails, inclusive of the
"way" which it has opened up. Since this "way" is necessarily
fraught with afflictions, it is "right" (*dikaion*; legal, legally right,
righteous in a court of law, and thus ultimately in God's eyes)
that they, his co-sharers (*synkoinōnous*) in the grace, be in his
heart (*kardia*; Hebrew *leb*, which is the mind), with which he is
uttering his high-priestly prayer, while he is in fetters (*desmois*;
chains, imprisonment) awaiting the day when he will defend
(make the apology [*apologia*] of) the gospel. However, the
Philippians ought not to worry: this defense is assured of being
successful (*bebaiōsei*) since the apology of the gospel cannot fail.
Indeed, it is God himself, a higher authority than the Roman
court, who will ensure its success. What Paul wrote to the
Corinthians applies to the Philippians as well: "... who [God]
will sustain you (*bebaiōsei*) to the end, guiltless in the day of our
Lord Jesus Christ. God is faithful, by whom you were called into
the fellowship (*koinōnian*) of his Son, Jesus Christ our Lord." (1
Cor 1:8-9)[22]

V. 8-11 ⁸μάρτυς γάρ μου ὁ θεός ὡς ἐπιποθῶ πάντας ὑμᾶς ἐν
σπλάγχνοις Χριστοῦ Ἰησοῦ. ⁹Καὶ τοῦτο προσεύχομαι, ἵνα ἡ
ἀγάπη ὑμῶν ἔτι μᾶλλον καὶ μᾶλλον περισσεύῃ ἐν ἐπιγνώσει
καὶ πάσῃ αἰσθήσει ¹⁰εἰς τὸ δοκιμάζειν ὑμᾶς τὰ διαφέροντα,
ἵνα ἦτε εἰλικρινεῖς καὶ ἀπρόσκοποι εἰς ἡμέραν Χριστοῦ,
¹¹πεπληρωμένοι καρπὸν δικαιοσύνης τὸν διὰ Ἰησοῦ Χριστοῦ
εἰς δόξαν καὶ ἔπαινον θεοῦ.

---

[22] Notice the similarity in thought as well as terminology with Philippians. Another
pertinent passage is 2 Cor 1:18-22: "As surely as God is faithful, our word to you has
not been Yes and No. For the Son of God, Jesus Christ, whom we preached among
you, Silvanus and Timothy and I, was not Yes and No; but in him it is always Yes. For
all the promises of God find their Yes in him. That is why we utter the Amen through
him, to the glory of God. But it is God who establishes (*bebaiōn*) us with you in
Christ, and has commissioned us; he has put his seal upon us and given us his Spirit in
our hearts as a guarantee."

⁸For God is my witness, how I yearn for you all with the affection of Christ Jesus. ⁹And it is my prayer that your love may abound more and more, with knowledge and all discernment, ¹⁰so that you may approve what is excellent, and may be pure and blameless for the day of Christ, ¹¹filled with the fruits of righteousness which come through Jesus Christ, to the glory and praise of God.

With Philippians 1:8 Paul continues to prepare his addressees for his eventual death. After having told them that he had them in his heart while in chains, he calls upon God as witness— implying that he is telling them the truth—that, beyond his heart, he actually yearns for them with the "entrails" (*splankhnois*) of Christ Jesus. This Greek word is found twice in the LXX, once as translation of the Hebrew *beten* (belly; Prov 26:22) and the other time of *rahamim* (entrails, womb; Prov 12:10). When compared to *leb* (core; heart), which is the center and thus the mind, the womb is the seat of the (motherly) instinct of affection toward the little child. This can be seen in that *rahamim* (plural of *rehem* [womb]) is usually translated into "mercy" or "compassion."[23] Hence the verb *splankhnizomai* (to feel with one's entrails, womb) is usually translated as "have compassion or pity" (Mt 15:32; 18:27; 20:34; Mk 1:41; 8:2; 9:22). Sometimes the Greek makes the meaning clear by using the explanatory phrase *splankhna eleou* (entrails of mercy; translated as "tender mercy" in RSV Lk 1:78) or *splankhna*

---

[23] In Hebrew, the plural of a term that is essentially singular, such as womb or blood, denotes that organ in action or live. Thus, *damim* (bloods) refer to the flowing blood (flow of blood, bloodstream) as compared to *dam* (blood) denoting the blood in general and thus can be used to refer to the non-flowing blood in a dead organism. The same applies to the "womb": the singular would refer to the organ itself, while the plural denotes this organ as a center of feeling. It corresponds to a mother's saying her child, "I carry you in my womb(s)."

oiktirmou (entrails of compassion; translated as "compassion" in RSV Col 3:12). So, Paul moves from his own heart to the divine mercy which God expressed through Christ Jesus. By doing so, Paul is leading the Philippians away from his person and concentrating rather on God's care for them through Christ Jesus. By the same token, he is preparing for the pressure he will be putting on them when he will ask them to behave according to *splankhna kai oiktirmoi* (mercy and compassion; Phil 2:1).[24] Indeed, already here, he says that his prayer before God is that they abound more and more in their love, which he will mention together with "mercy and compassion" (Phil 2:1). Here, we can see very clearly that Paul's gospel does not boil down to a (correct) creed formula; rather, it is God's law by which all are to abide, including the Gentiles (Rom 2:11-16), and which is subsumed in the love of the neighbor (Rom 13:9-10; Gal 5:13-14). And since it is this gospel of love for the neighbor that will be the muster by which all will be judged (Rom 2:16), Paul adds that the Philippians ought not only to abide by it, but also to abound in it, so that they "be pure and blameless for the day of Christ." Nothing less will do since the work which is done in and by them is God's (Phil 1:6; 2:12-13).

What then is the function of knowledge? Beginning with the second century, interest among the church leaders was overtaken by philosophy and intellectual discourse. Since that time, Christian thought has been influenced by philosophical terminology whereby knowledge is expressed as being mental. This has often led to the misinterpretation of scripture by making out of it essentially a source for information so that we

_____

tion and sympathy" in RSV.

end up with the correct formula of belief.[25] The result is that what takes the place of primacy is no longer the text, and thus what God says, but what we think of it, as though God's word is an invitation to intellectual debate *à la* Plato's dialogues or philosophical treatises. Knowledge in scripture is knowledge of God's law, which are commandments expressing his will. They are given to us, and we are to know them *in order to do them*, as we hear repeatedly especially in Deuteronomy.[26] This explains why in scripture the people are accused of not knowing the Law and even not knowing God himself when they do not abide by his will. An investigation of Paul's terminology in Philippians 1:9-10 will corroborate this. First and foremost, it would be non-Pauline, if not outright anti-Pauline, to say that one's love for the neighbor would abound more and more when one is filled with theoretical knowledge and discernment. Being bred in scripture, Paul actually denigrates human (Gentile) wisdom (1 Cor 1:22-25) and castigates the Gentiles' behavior of ultimately not doing God's will as the sign of their lack of knowledge of him:

> And since they [the Gentiles] did not see fit (*edokimasan*; discerned)[27] to acknowledge (*ekhein en epignōsei*;[28] hold knowledge of) God, God gave them up to a base (*adokimon*; undiscerning)[29] mind and to improper conduct (*poiein*; doing). They were filled with all manner of wickedness, evil, covetousness, malice. Full of

---

[25] This phenomenon is at its clearest when it comes to interpreting the so-called "Christological passages" such as Phil 2:5-11, which we shall be discussing further below.

[26] That is why Wisdom literature invites the nations to recognize that God's law *is* actually the expression of true wisdom (and knowledge that it entails) which the nations are yearning and looking for. See *OTI₃* 129-141.

[27] Which is the same verb *dokimazein* found in Phil 1:10.

[28] The same noun Paul uses in Phil 1:9.

[29] From the same root as the verb *dokimazein*.

envy, murder, strife, deceit, malignity, they are gossips, slanderers, haters of God, insolent, haughty, boastful, inventors of evil, disobedient to parents, foolish, faithless, heartless, ruthless. Though they know (*epignontes*)[30] God's decree (*dikaiōma*; statute, righteous utterance) that those who do (*prassontes*; practice) such things deserve to die, they not only do (*poiousin*) them but approve those who practice (*prassousin*) them. (Rom 1:28-32)

Against false knowledge (of intellectual discourse) Paul proposes the true knowledge of God's will in his law. Then, in order to drive home his point, he critiques with the same harshness the Jew who has (knows the content of) the Law and yet does not *do* its precepts:

Therefore you have no excuse, O man, whoever you are, when you judge another; for in passing judgment upon him you condemn yourself, because you, the judge, are doing (*prasseis*; practicing) the very same things. We know that the judgment of God rightly falls upon those who do (*prassontas*; practice) such things. Do you suppose, O man, that when you judge those who do (*prassontas*; practice) such things and yet do (*poiōn*) them yourself, you will escape the judgment of God? (2:1-3)

Yet, Paul does not conclude as we often do, "What is the use of God's law and oracles if they are not obeyed?" Rather, he upholds them since our salvation lies in abiding by them:

Then what advantage has the Jew? Or what is the value of circumcision? Much in every way. To begin with, the Jews are entrusted with the oracles of God. What if some were unfaithful? Does their faithlessness nullify the faithfulness of God? By no means! Let God be true though every man be false, as it is written, "That thou mayest be justified in thy words, and prevail when thou art judged." (3:1-4)

---

[30] This verb is from the same root as the noun *epignōsei*.

So the law is holy, and the commandment is holy and just and good ... We know that the law is spiritual; but I am carnal, sold under sin. (7:12, 14)

In Colossians, a letter closely related to Philippians, we have at its clearest the interconnection between (the) knowledge (of God's law) and love (expressed in every good work):

And so, from the day we heard of it, we have not ceased to pray for you, asking that you may be filled with the knowledge (*epignōsin*) *of his will* in all spiritual wisdom and understanding, *to lead a life* worthy of the Lord, fully pleasing to him, *bearing fruit in every good work and increasing in the knowledge* (epignōsei) *of God.* (Col 1:9-10)[31]

In Philippians 1:9, Paul actually explains what he means by "knowledge" by adding "all discernment (*aisthēsei*)" with the aim of "approving (testing) what is excellent (better; different)." The two other instances of the root *aisth*— in the New Testament shed light on its meaning. The first parallels the terminology of our text in that it includes in the same statement the root *gno*— (knowledge): "But they did not understand (*ēgnooun*) this saying, and it was concealed from them, that they should not perceive (*aisthōntai*) it; and they were afraid to ask him about this saying." (Lk 9:45) Thus, the root *aisth*— seems to have the connotation of (deeper) perception and may reflect the quality discernment and, if so, it both underscores the meaning and heightens the level of "knowledge."[32] The other occurrence sheds even more

---

[31] See also Philem 4-6 (I thank my God always when I remember you in my prayers, because I hear of your *love* and of the faith which you have toward the Lord Jesus and all the saints, and I pray that the sharing [*koinōnia*] of your faith may become effective [*energēs*; from the same root as *ergon*— work] the knowledge (*epignōsei*) of all the *good* that is ours in Christ).

[32] This may explain the addition of "all" (*pasē*) before "discernment" (with knowledge and all discernment) in Phil 1:9.

light on our Philippians text because it uses another term that clearly means discernment and stresses that the choice is on the level of doing, more specifically distinguishing and thus choosing between good and evil: "But solid food is for the mature, for those who have their faculties (*aisthētēria*) trained by practice to distinguish (*diakrisin*) good from evil." (Heb 5:14) This is precisely the function of *aisthēsei* in Philippians: to "approve (*dokimazein*; test in order to discern and distinguish) (and thus choose) what is excellent (*ta diapheronta*; the different, better, more suitable matters)" (1:10) in view of the judgment. Finally, the clear intent of Philippians 1:9-10 is not so much to invite the addressees to adhere to mentally correct knowledge, but rather to *live* according to God's will as expressed in his commandments. This is corroborated in Romans 2:17-20 where we read:

> But if you call yourself a Jew and rely upon the law and boast of your relation to God and *know* his *will* and *approve what is excellent* (*dokimazeis ta diapheronta*), because you are instructed in the *law*, and if *you are sure* (*pepoithas*) that you are a guide to the blind, a light to those who are in darkness, a corrector of the foolish, a teacher of children, having in the law the embodiment of *knowledge* and truth...

Compare with Philippians:

> And I am sure (*pepoithōs*) ... And it is my prayer that your love may abound more and more, with *knowledge* and all discernment, so that you may *approve what is excellent* (*dokimazein ta diapheronta*), and may be pure and blameless for the day of Christ, filled with the fruits of righteousness which come through Jesus Christ, to the glory and praise of God. (1:5, 9-11)

The Philippians are to keep testing and thus choosing what is excellent from the perspective of the divine judgment. Their state of purity and blamelessness will be vindicated when and if they are declared "righteous" (*dikaioi*; innocent of any wrongdoing in the Law's eyes). However, their righteousness or the lack thereof will be judged on whether they will have borne the fruit (singular in the original Greek) that expresses such righteousness. One ought not to conclude that "fruit" and "fruits" bear different connotations. A comparison between the parallel passages Mt 7:15-17, where the plural is used, and Lk 6:43-45, which has the singular, should be convincing enough in this regard. The singular may refer to the harvest. In the case here, this may well be the intention since the Philippians are asked to be "filled" (*peplērōmenoi*) with such. Since the verb *plēroō* (fill; bring to fulfillment) corresponds in meaning to *epiteleō* (complete, accomplish; 1:6), it is God who in the end is the producer of the harvest; hence glory and praise are due him. He will, indeed, consider us "righteous" through sheer grace, and not because of anything we have or shall have done. The fruit of righteousness is accomplished "through (God's servant) Jesus Christ," and Paul will explain later in Philippians 3:4-14, how this takes place and how the "good work" (1:6) or "fruit" (v.11) we must produce is the effect of divine grace.

Vv. 12-18 ¹²Γινώσκειν δὲ ὑμᾶς βούλομαι, ἀδελφοί, ὅτι τὰ κατ᾽ ἐμὲ μᾶλλον εἰς προκοπὴν τοῦ εὐαγγελίου ἐλήλυθεν, ¹³ὥστε τοὺς δεσμούς μου φανεροὺς ἐν Χριστῷ γενέσθαι ἐν ὅλῳ τῷ πραιτωρίῳ καὶ τοῖς λοιποῖς πᾶσιν, ¹⁴καὶ τοὺς πλείονας τῶν ἀδελφῶν ἐν κυρίῳ πεποιθότας τοῖς δεσμοῖς μου περισσοτέρως τολμᾶν ἀφόβως τὸν λόγον λαλεῖν. ¹⁵τινὲς μὲν καὶ διὰ φθόνον καὶ ἔριν, τινὲς δὲ καὶ δι᾽ εὐδοκίαν τὸν Χριστὸν κηρύσσουσιν· ¹⁶οἱ μὲν ἐξ ἀγάπης, εἰδότες ὅτι εἰς ἀπολογίαν τοῦ εὐαγγελίου κεῖμαι, ¹⁷οἱ δὲ ἐξ ἐριθείας τὸν Χριστὸν καταγγέλλουσιν, οὐχ ἁγνῶς, οἰόμενοι θλῖψιν ἐγείρειν τοῖς δεσμοῖς μου. ¹⁸Τί γάρ; πλὴν ὅτι παντὶ τρόπῳ,

εἴτε προφάσει εἴτε ἀληθείᾳ, Χριστὸς καταγγέλλεται, καὶ ἐν
τούτῳ χαίρω. Ἀλλὰ καὶ χαρήσομαι,

*12I want you to know, brethren, that what has happened to me
has really served to advance the gospel, 13so that it has become
known throughout the whole praetorian guard and to all the
rest that my imprisonment is for Christ; 14and most of the
brethren have been made confident in the Lord because of my
imprisonment, and are much more bold to speak the word of
God without fear. 15Some indeed preach Christ from envy and
rivalry, but others from good will. 16The latter do it out of love,
knowing that I am put here for the defense of the gospel; 17the
former proclaim Christ out of partisanship, not sincerely but
thinking to afflict me in my imprisonment. 18What then? Only
that in every way, whether in pretense or in truth, Christ is
proclaimed; and in that I rejoice. Yes, and I shall rejoice.*

Before offering Jesus Christ as an example for the Philippians to
follow (2:6-11), Paul gives himself as an example of the obedient
slave (1:12-24). As he established in 1:5 (thankful for your
partnership in the gospel from the first day until now), the
bridge between him and the Philippians is the gospel: "I want
you to know, brethren, that what has happened to me has really
served to advance the gospel." (v.12) What matters after all is the
steady advancement (*prokopēn*; progress, furtherance) of the
gospel between the point of its beginning and the completion of
its work by God (v.6). What Paul has in mind while writing this
verse is obvious; he wants the Philippians to be "blameless"
(*aproskopoi*) on judgment day (v.10). Both *prokopē* and
aproskopoi are from the same root *koptō* (cut). With the prefix *pro*
(ahead, before) it has the connotation of moving forward,
cutting one's way ahead, whereas with the preposition *pros*
(toward) it has the connotation of moving toward and thus

cutting in, blocking the course, being a scandal, causing to stumble, hindering.[33] The other two instances of the adjective *aproskop*—refer to either people (1 Cor 10:32) or a conscience (Acts 24:16) that do not scandalize or are not offensive to others.[34] So here, in Philippians, Paul is asking his addressees to follow in his footsteps by behaving in a way that would not be a hindrance to the spread of the gospel message.

How does Paul show that he has not been and hopes never to be a hindrance to the gospel? First he asserts that what happened to him *until now* was for the furtherance of the gospel. While in prison awaiting judgment by the governor's court when he would be allowed to make his "apology" (Phil 1:7), word spread among the guards and through them to the entire Roman praetorium (governor's quarters) in Ephesus that the reason behind his imprisonment is the teaching he is promoting, which is the gospel message. Consequently, the gospel message became known in the praetorium. Thus his jailing is for the sake of Christ as preached by him, since for the Ephesian hearers there is no Christ except the one that came out of Paul's mouth. The inevitable corollary is that Paul, though a Roman citizen, was actually the slave not of Caesar but of Christ and a "citizen" not of the Roman commonwealth (*politevma*; polity) but of Christ's commonwealth (3:20). Not only that, the gospel word is spreading even faster due to Paul's imprisonment since many of the brethren are emboldened to "take over," so to speak (1:14). To prepare for his statement in vv.15-18 that it is so, the intention notwithstanding, he says that all the brethren who

---

[33] *proskomma* (Rom 9:32, 33: 14:13, 20) and *proskopē* (2 Cor 6:3) are the nouns.
[34] Both these cases are actually intimately related to Philippians.

"took over" did so as daringly as himself,[35] because they were "confident" (*pepoithotas*; convinced, assured, secure) just as Paul was "sure" (*pepoithōs*; sure, v.6) regarding the fulfillment of the gospel (vv.5-6).

This is where Paul's attitude is stunning. Instead of judging intentions, which is the usual trap most, if not all of us, fall into, he considers judgment solely God's domain on the last day and concentrates instead on the fact that God is always in control. Indeed, if Caesar himself cannot control the furtherance of the gospel, which is taking place in spite of the chains Caesar put on the message's promoter, then much less can the intentions of regular humans affect that furtherance. The result is that the gospel's—Paul's—Christ is being preached regardless of any intentions, be they envy and rivalry (*erin*) or goodwill and good feelings, be they partisanship (rivalry; *eritheias*) or love.[36] The first group referred to are those who act out of partisanship (v.17; rivalry) in order to produce envy and, consequently, more rivalry. This, they presume, is going to bring more affliction on Paul[37] and, as was the case in Corinth,[38] split the church of

---

[35] Notice the parallelism in meaning between "are much more bold (*tolman*) to speak the word of God without fear (*aphobōs*)" (1:14) and "with full courage (*parrhēsia*; boldness)" (v.20).

[36] I am reading the preposition *dia* in 1:15 as "for the sake of, with a view to"—which is its usual connotation when followed by an accusative—rather then "from." This seems to be the better solution for two reasons. On the one hand, later in its other occurrence in Philippians the "goodwill (pleasure)" (*evdokias*) is God's: "for God is at work in you, both to will and to work for his good pleasure." (2:13) On the other hand, the same thought of 1:15 is repeated in the following verses (16-17) with the preposition *ex* (out of, from).

[37] The envious ones can only presume to add affliction since the affliction in Paul's perspective is linked to the gospel (Phil 1:16) for whose sake Paul is already undergoing the affliction of imprisonment.

[38] 1 Cor 1:11 (For it has been reported to me by Chloe's people that there is quarreling [*erides*; quarrelings] among you, my brethren); 3:3 (for you are still of the flesh. For

Philippi for whose unity Paul has struggled and is still struggling. The other group is those who know God's "goodwill" and act according to it; God's will is subsumed in the commandment of love that builds up the community as one body. Still, Paul is not worried for in pretense or in truth the gospel's Christ is proclaimed, and this proclamation is willed by the God who will see to it that what he started is brought to full fruition (v.6). And it is precisely in this conviction, but also in hope (v.20), that Paul rejoices and will continue to rejoice; the joy is after all that of the coming kingdom of the heavenly Jerusalem. By not issuing his own judgment, Paul is relegating the final word of judgment to the coming Lord who will determine the fate of all.

Vv. 19-26 ¹⁹οἶδα γὰρ ὅτι τοῦτό μοι ἀποβήσεται εἰς σωτηρίαν διὰ τῆς ὑμῶν δεήσεως καὶ ἐπιχορηγίας τοῦ πνεύματος Ἰησοῦ Χριστοῦ ²⁰κατὰ τὴν ἀποκαραδοκίαν καὶ ἐλπίδα μου, ὅτι ἐν οὐδενὶ αἰσχυνθήσομαι ἀλλ᾽ ἐν πάσῃ παρρησίᾳ ὡς πάντοτε καὶ νῦν μεγαλυνθήσεται Χριστὸς ἐν τῷ σώματί μου, εἴτε διὰ ζωῆς εἴτε διὰ θανάτου. ²¹Ἐμοὶ γὰρ τὸ ζῆν Χριστὸς καὶ τὸ ἀποθανεῖν κέρδος. ²²εἰ δὲ τὸ ζῆν ἐν σαρκί, τοῦτό μοι καρπὸς ἔργου, καὶ τί αἱρήσομαι οὐ γνωρίζω. ²³συνέχομαι δὲ ἐκ τῶν δύο, τὴν ἐπιθυμίαν ἔχων εἰς τὸ ἀναλῦσαι καὶ σὺν Χριστῷ εἶναι, πολλῷ [γὰρ] μᾶλλον κρεῖσσον· ²⁴τὸ δὲ ἐπιμένειν [ἐν] τῇ σαρκὶ ἀναγκαιότερον δι᾽ ὑμᾶς. ²⁵καὶ τοῦτο πεποιθὼς οἶδα ὅτι μενῶ καὶ παραμενῶ πᾶσιν ὑμῖν εἰς τὴν ὑμῶν προκοπὴν καὶ χαρὰν τῆς πίστεως, ²⁶ἵνα τὸ καύχημα ὑμῶν περισσεύῃ ἐν Χριστῷ Ἰησοῦ ἐν ἐμοὶ διὰ τῆς ἐμῆς παρουσίας πάλιν πρὸς ὑμᾶς.

¹⁹For I know that through your prayers and the help of the Spirit of Jesus Christ this will turn out for my deliverance, ²⁰as it is my eager expectation and hope that I shall not be at all ashamed,

---

while there is jealousy and strife (*eris*) among you, are you not of the flesh, and behaving like ordinary men?).

but that with full courage now as always Christ will be honored in my body, whether by life or by death. ²¹For to me to live is Christ, and to die is gain. ²²If it is to be life in the flesh, that means fruitful labor for me. Yet which I shall choose I cannot tell. ²³I am hard pressed between the two. My desire is to depart and be with Christ, for that is far better. ²⁴But to remain in the flesh is more necessary on your account. ²⁵Convinced of this, I know that I shall remain and continue with you all, for your progress and joy in the faith, ²⁶so that in me you may have ample cause to glory in Christ Jesus, because of my coming to you again.

Paul's assuredness in regard to the gospel and its ultimate success is to prepare the Philippians for any eventuality: his release from prison or his demise. He does so by using the term "salvation" (*sōtērian*; deliverance). Salvation is essentially imperial terminology since one of the imperial titles is that of "savior" (*sōtēr*). To render the content of his gospel understandable to his Gentiles, most of whom were slaves, Paul launched the use of this same term in conjunction with the salvation God has in store for them through Jesus Christ. God's Christ was condemned by the Roman authorities and thus appeared not to have secured salvation for himself and, by extension, for his followers (as an emperor would); yet the scriptural God vindicated him as the true "lord" (emperor) and thus the means for everyone's true salvation (2:9-11). By assuring the Philippians that "I know that ... this (his present situation) will turn out for my deliverance" (1:18), Paul becomes a winner on either count: whether he will be released from prison by Caesar, through the governor of the province Asia, or by the decision that he be executed. The reason for Paul's assurance is simple: as the slave of his only master, the Christ of God, Paul is under the latter's authority in whatever he wills. And, for Paul, God is definitely in control since he is able to secure the progress of the gospel in spite of the governor's decision to imprison Paul. But, before explicating the how of the matter, Paul forces upon the Philippians acceptance of God's decision, whatever it might be, by including them in the process. What will turn out to be for his deliverance, he says, will not only be due to the work of the same Spirit through whom God fulfilled his work in Jesus Christ, but also due to the Philippians' prayers for Paul's deliverance.

Paul looks ahead to his salvation with an eagerness anchored in an assured hope that God who started his plan will bring it to completion. He thus knows that he will not be put to shame on judgment day. He is actually filled with the same "boldness" (*parrhēsia*; courage) that brought him to his current state of imprisonment. And there is no reason for shame since the gospel's Christ who has been until now (as always; *hōs pantote*) honored through the gospel word, will also now (*kai nyn*) be honored (*megalynthēsetai*; magnified) *in Paul's body* whether he remains alive or he dies. The reason is straightforward: living (*to zēn*; the act or reality of living) is the Christ as he had preached him and, consequently, dying (*to apothanein*; the act or reality of dying) is a gain (1:21). That is to say, if he ends up living, then he will continue doing what he has been doing all along, preaching Christ in the same way. This is the unavoidable commission that is imposed on him (1 Cor 9:16-17), and his master will grant him life so long as he is carrying out this commission in obedience. If he dies—that is his hope—then at the resurrection unto judgment, he will be shown to have died due to the same obedience and his "lowly body" will be like Christ's "glorious body" (3:21).

However, this is not as simple as it appears. Paul will discuss the "gain" (in death) more extensively later in 3:4-11. Here, he goes to the heart of the matter: love for the others, which is factually the gospel. Obedience of the slave to his lord lies in following his orders, which in the gospel boils down to giving priority to the needs of others over our own yearnings, lest these yearnings become "the desires of our flesh" which "are against the Spirit" (Gal 5:17) whom Paul just referred to as "the Spirit of (the lord) Jesus Christ" (Phil 1:19). Indeed, although at the surface it looks as a losing proposition, "living (*to zēn*) in the flesh" (v.22)—for the sake of the Philippians as he explains later (v.24)—is an opportunity for more "fruitful labor" (*karpos ergou*) in the gospel.[39] This explains why Paul is not actually eager to opt for dying and being with Christ (vv.22-24). He may not, after all, inherit the kingdom if it is discovered that he did so for an easy, quick gain! To the contrary, he is "convinced" (*pepoithōs*) with the same conviction as the one connected with his gospel (v.6) that he will not die; rather "I know that I shall remain and continue with you all, for your progress[40] and joy[41] in the faith[42]" (v.25). Indeed, the joy of the coming kingdom is one that is to be—actually cannot but be—shared between the

---

[39] See 1:6 (And I am sure that he who began a *good work* in you will bring it to completion at the day of Jesus Christ) and 1:9-11 (And it is my prayer that your love may abound more and more, with knowledge and all discernment, so that you may approve what is excellent, and may be pure and blameless for the day of Christ, filled with the *fruits of righteousness* which come through Jesus Christ, to the glory and praise of God) and my comments on these verses above.

[40] This progress (*prokopē*) is none other than that of the gospel (v.12).

[41] This joy is none other than the eschatological joy linked to the progress and fruition of the gospel (vv.15-19).

[42] This "faith" of the Philippians is none other than their trust in the word of the gospel, which trust sustains them to proceed on the way ending in the kingdom and its joy.

sower and the reaper.[43] This is precisely what Paul states in his conclusion: "so that in me you may have ample cause to glory in Christ Jesus, because of my coming to you again." (v.26)

This statement is intentionally triple edged. First, Paul's coming again to the Philippians refers, at face value, to his release from prison. Such will give them ample cause to find reason to feel pride (*kavkhēma*; glory) in (the lord) Christ Jesus who was able to save his slave Paul from death. Second, the Philippians' boasting is said to "abound" (*perissevē*), which is the same verb that Paul used of their love in his prayer for them (v.9). Thus, their boasting in Christ Jesus, whose reason is Paul, can be due to their realization that the "lord" succeeded to subdue his "slave" into abiding by his rule of the love for the other and even made this love "abound."   Third, in case Paul is actually sentenced to death after having written the letter, he will have proven that it was after all his love for the Philippians that guided his preference and thus he will have proven to be worthy of inheriting the Kingdom. This in turn will make Paul part of Christ's retinue at his coming and the Philippians who "will have been left behind" will witness such,[44] which will give them a sense of pride regarding their apostle. This third meaning is borne by Paul's use of "coming" (*parousias*) which is a technical term referring to the Lord's coming in glory. The extra connotation is corroborated by that later, in 2:16, Paul says that he would feel the same "boasting" on the Lord's (judgment) day if the Philippians will have held fast to the "word of life," a sign that Paul himself will have stayed the course of the gospel: "[that you may be] holding fast the word of life, so that in the day of

---

[43] Jn 4:36.
[44] 1 Thess 4:13-17.

Christ I may be proud (*eis kavkhēma emoi*) that I did not run in vain or labor in vain."

So actually, before getting to the point where he would reveal to them that, most probably, they will not see him again, Paul has already committed to writing the "gospel" he will be asking them to abide by. Put otherwise, it is the letter to the Philippians itself that *is* Paul's gospel, the sole gospel, the one that was from the beginning and will remain until the end. It is only by hearing the letter read to them that every generation encounters *for the first time* the gospel. And what applies to Philippians applies equally to each and every book of the New Testament. It is in each and every one of his letters that Paul is heard saying: "My little children, with whom I am *again* in travail until Christ be formed in you!" (Gal 4:19) Every time we hear scripture we are being borne, and thus born, "again." Anything else, before, after or even parallel to scripture *as it is written*, any "variation in wording," is potentially harmful as Paul authoritatively states in 2 Corinthians:

> I wish you would bear with me in a little foolishness. Do bear with me! I feel a divine jealousy for you, for I betrothed you to Christ to present you as a pure bride to her one husband. But I am afraid that as the serpent deceived Eve by his cunning, your thoughts will be led astray from a sincere and pure devotion to Christ. For if some one comes and preaches *another Jesus than the one we preached*, or if you receive a different spirit from the one you received, or if you accept a different gospel from the one you accepted, you submit to it readily enough … And what I do I will continue to do, in order to undermine the claim of those who would like to claim that in their boasted mission they work on the same terms as we do. For such men are false apostles, deceitful workmen, disguising themselves as apostles of Christ. And no wonder, for even Satan disguises himself as an angel of light. So it

is not strange if his servants also disguise themselves as servants of righteousness. Their end will correspond to their deeds. (11:1-4, 12-15)

What Paul is writing or what is being written in his name is already being written against a perverted rendition of his gospel. So this time he commits his original gospel to writing "with his own hand" (Gal 6:10) in order that it not be changed or perverted again:

> I am astonished that you are so quickly deserting him who called you in the grace of Christ and turning to a different gospel—not that there is another gospel, but there are some who trouble you and want to pervert the gospel of Christ. But even if we, or an angel from heaven, should preach to you a gospel contrary to that which we preached to you, let him be accursed. As we have said before, so now I say again, If any one is preaching to you a gospel contrary to that which you received, let him be accursed. (Gal 1:6-9)

Consequently, as it becomes clear from Philippians 1:3-26, the Pauline gospel is the solely valid one. It is not some kind of an ethereal reality or even a correct statement, but rather a practical teaching challenging us to obey a lord who saved us and put us under his wing and commanded us to love unconditionally anyone who is in need of us. This is the gospel teaching that is iterated in so many different literary ways in the letters of Paul and, by extension, in the books of the New Testament. Each New Testament book is the full gospel and not some kind of a proof text from which we pick and choose in order to formulate our version of the "original" gospel. The admonishments as well as the exhortations included in the letters are an integral part of the gospel that is a teaching, an instruction, we have to obey and not debate intellectually. What actually makes the Pauline gospel ominous is that it is simple to understand but hard to follow!

Vv. 27-30 ²⁷ Μόνον ἀξίως τοῦ εὐαγγελίου τοῦ Χριστοῦ πολιτεύεσθε, ἵνα εἴτε ἐλθὼν καὶ ἰδὼν ὑμᾶς εἴτε ἀπὼν ἀκούω τὰ περὶ ὑμῶν, ὅτι στήκετε ἐν ἑνὶ πνεύματι, μιᾷ ψυχῇ συναθλοῦντες τῇ πίστει τοῦ εὐαγγελίου ²⁸καὶ μὴ πτυρόμενοι ἐν μηδενὶ ὑπὸ τῶν ἀντικειμένων, ἥτις ἐστὶν αὐτοῖς ἔνδειξις ἀπωλείας, ὑμῶν δὲ σωτηρίας, καὶ τοῦτο ἀπὸ θεοῦ· ²⁹ὅτι ὑμῖν ἐχαρίσθη τὸ ὑπὲρ Χριστοῦ, οὐ μόνον τὸ εἰς αὐτὸν πιστεύειν ἀλλὰ καὶ τὸ ὑπὲρ αὐτοῦ πάσχειν, ³⁰τὸν αὐτὸν ἀγῶνα ἔχοντες, οἷον εἴδετε ἐν ἐμοὶ καὶ νῦν ἀκούετε ἐν ἐμοί.

> *²⁷Only let your manner of life be worthy of the gospel of Christ, so that whether I come and see you or am absent, I may hear of you that you stand firm in one spirit, with one mind striving side by side for the faith of the gospel, ²⁸and not frightened in anything by your opponents. This is a clear omen to them of their destruction, but of your salvation, and that from God. ²⁹For it has been granted to you that for the sake of Christ you should not only believe in him but also suffer for his sake, ³⁰engaged in the same conflict which you saw and now hear to be mine.*

My understanding of what the Pauline gospel is all about is corroborated in this passage of the epistle. <u>All the aforesaid, says Paul, has no value "unless" (*monon*; only) the Philippians act worthily of their new citizenship into which the Apostle has just borne them.</u> They are to behave according to his teaching whether he is present or absent. The reason is that, when absent, he will hear of their behavior, and thus they always run the risk of hearing his condemnation as in 1 Corinthians 5:1-5. What the Apostle would want to hear is that they are "standing firm in one spirit, with one mind, striving side by side through (while

putting) their trust in the gospel (teaching, requirements)."[45]
Only if one misreads *pistei* as meaning "a creed formula" and not
according to its original connotation of "trusting" will one end
up differentiating between the two aspects of the gospel: a
practical one requiring a certain behavior and a theoretical
formulaic one. The terminology, however, does not bear such a
dichotomy.

That the gospel teaching is a torah, a behavioral instruction
one is to follow, can be seen in the imagery of the race that is
frequently associated with the gospel in the Pauline corpus and
which is found here. As early as Galatians where Paul set the
tone of his defense of "the truth of the gospel" (2:5, 14), we hear
him using the imagery of running in reference to the
commitment to the gospel required of the Galatians (You were
running well; who hindered you from obeying [*peithesthai*;
trusting, relying on, being confident of] the truth? 5:7) as well as
to his own apostolic activity (I went up by revelation; and I laid
before them—but privately before those who were of repute—
the gospel which I preach among the Gentiles, lest somehow I
should be running or had run in vain; 2:2). This running is that
performed at a race:

> I do it all for the sake of the gospel, that I may share in its
> blessings. Do you not know that in a race (*en stadiō*; in a
> stadium[46]) all the runners compete, but only one receives the
> prize? So run that you may obtain it. Every athlete (*agōnizomenos*)
> exercises self-control in all things. They do it to receive a
> perishable wreath, but we an imperishable. Well, I do not run
> aimlessly, I do not box as one beating the air; but I pommel my

---

[45] RSV has "for the faith of the gospel."
[46] It referred to a foot race that took place, during the Olympic and other Panhellenic Games, in a building called *stadion* (*stadium* in Latin).

body and subdue it, lest after preaching to others I myself should
be disqualified. (1 Cor 9:23-27)

The Greek word translated into "athlete" (in RSV 1 Cor 9:25) is
from the same root as the noun *agōna* translated as conflict (in
RSV Phil 1:30). Actually the Greek *agōn* referred to the arena
where athletic competitions took place and, only by extension,
came to mean also the effort that athletes put into such.

Philippians 1:27-30 is then to be understood from the same
perspective. Paul is giving himself as an example for his hearers
to follow by having them join in the same race as he: "engaged in
the same conflict (*agōna*; athletic competition, more specifically
race) which you saw and now hear to be mine." (v.30) One
undertakes such a race because one has put one's trust in the
God that set both Paul and the Philippians on that race's path
(v.6), a trust that the same God will help them finish it.
However, since Paul's example has shown that such a path
includes suffering (vv.7-17), the Philippians are invited to
understand that this is also their fate: "For it has been granted
(*ekharisthē*; it has been given by [God's] grace) to you that for
the sake of Christ you should not only trust in him but also
suffer for his sake." (v.29) And they have no choice but to
proceed on this path whose beginning, as is clear from the
reference to grace, coincides with that of the reception of Paul's
gospel (v.5).

Running a given path brings to mind the verb "walk" which is
Paul's favorite when speaking of behavior.[47] This is confirmed by

---

[47] See for example Gal 5:16 (But I say, walk by the Spirit, and do not gratify the
desires of the flesh); Rom 6:4 (so that ... we too might walk in newness of life); Rom
8:4 (in order that the just requirement of the law might be fulfilled in us, who walk
not according to the flesh but according to the Spirit.). Actually, it is my contention
that out of all athletic competitions, Paul's preference for the imagery of race to speak

what he writes later when he again gives himself as an example to follow:

> Brethren, join in imitating me, and mark those who so walk (*peripatountas*) as you have an example in us. For many, of whom I have often told you and now tell you even with tears, walk (*peripatousin*) as enemies of the cross of Christ. Their end is destruction[48] ... (3:17-19)

So, the question remains: "What would such behavior consist of?" An analysis of the terminology in this passage and the following will readily show that it is the usual Pauline barometer, love for the neighbor. The main point of Philippians 1:27 is togetherness. In order for the Philippians to "act as citizens (members of a polity, commonwealth)" (*politevesthe*), they are asked to "stand firm in one spirit, with one mind striving side by side (*synathlountes*) in their trust in the gospel (teaching)." The verb *synathleō* (act as athletes together) not only goes hand in hand with the imagery of the race (*agōna*) in v.30, but it also denotes the attitude that is reflected in a relay race, where all the runners are to work together. It is in such a way that Paul is asking the Philippians to stand firm. Later we shall see that the same verb *synathleō* (4:3)[49] is used to speak of the unity required among Jews and Gentiles in the community. The other way to stress togetherness is through the phrases "in *one* spirit" and "with *one* mind (*psykhē*; soul, breath)," meaning "as one (team)" by submitting one's own being to the will of God's spirit. The immediately following passage (2:1-5), which incorporates this

---

of the gospel and its requirements has to do with its connection with "walking" the path of the *torah*.

[48] Compare "*enemies* of the cross of Christ. Their end is *destruction*" with "and not frightened in anything by your *opponents*. This is a clear omen to them of their *destruction*" (1:28).

[49] It is the only other instance in the New Testament.

same terminology of "fellowship of the Spirit" (*koinōnia pnevmatos*) and "of the same mind" (*sympsykhoi*), revolves around the love for others required from the members of the Philippian community.

Chapter 2

Vv. 1-5 ¹ *Εἴ τις οὖν παράκλησις ἐν Χριστῷ, εἴ τι παραμύθιον ἀγάπης, εἴ τις κοινωνία πνεύματος, εἴ τις σπλάγχνα καὶ οἰκτιρμοί,* ²*πληρώσατέ μου τὴν χαρὰν ἵνα τὸ αὐτὸ φρονῆτε, τὴν αὐτὴν ἀγάπην ἔχοντες, σύμψυχοι, τὸ ἓν φρονοῦντες,* ³*μηδὲν κατ' ἐριθείαν μηδὲ κατὰ κενοδοξίαν ἀλλὰ τῇ ταπεινοφροσύνῃ ἀλλήλους ἡγούμενοι ὑπερέχοντας ἑαυτῶν,* ⁴*μὴ τὰ ἑαυτῶν ἕκαστος σκοποῦντες ἀλλὰ [καὶ] τὰ ἑτέρων ἕκαστοι.* ⁵*Τοῦτο φρονεῖτε ἐν ὑμῖν ὃ καὶ ἐν Χριστῷ Ἰησοῦ,*

¹So if there is any encouragement in Christ, any incentive of love, any participation in the Spirit, any affection and sympathy, ²complete my joy by being of the same mind, having the same love, being in full accord and of one mind. ³Do nothing from selfishness or conceit, but in humility count others better than yourselves. ⁴Let each of you look not only to his own interests, but also to the interests of others. ⁵Have this mind among yourselves, which is yours in Christ Jesus,

This passage plays a central role in the body of the epistle; in a sense the entire message of the epistle is subsumed in it. An analysis of these verses will show the veracity of this statement. By proceeding with "therefore," Paul makes of the following a conclusion based on the preceding chapter. However, what he actually does here is turn his description of true citizenry in the Kingdom into a command to abide by the commandment of unconditional love for the other. As he did in Galatians, he leaves this teaching in a written form, the epistle itself, so that the teaching would never be tampered with in the church of Philippi or in any other church that would eventually

99

hear the epistle read.[1]   The key phrase that brings all these
elements together is the start of the initial statement, "if there is
any encouragement (*paraklēsis*) in Christ."

The idea of *paraklēsis* in Paul has the technical meaning of
imparting an authoritative teaching of the Lord himself to the
community, a teaching with specific instructions to be followed.
This understanding is at its clearest in 1 Corinthians where
during the church gatherings the prophet is the preferred orator
over the speaker in tongues. This is because the prophet's words
edify the entire community and not just himself:

> Make love your aim, and earnestly desire the spiritual gifts,
> especially that you may prophesy. For one who speaks in a tongue
> speaks not to men but to God; for no one understands him, but
> he utters mysteries in the Spirit. On the other hand, he who
> prophesies speaks to men for their upbuilding (edification) and
> encouragement (*paraklēsin*) and consolation (*paramythian*). He
> who speaks in a tongue edifies himself, but he who prophesies
> edifies the church. Now I want you all to speak in tongues, but
> even more to prophesy. He who prophesies is greater than he who
> speaks in tongues, unless some one interprets, so that the church
> may be edified. Now, brethren, if I come to you speaking in
> tongues, how shall I benefit you unless I bring you some revelation
> or knowledge or prophecy or teaching? (1 Cor 14:1-6)

The closeness of the above passage with Philippians, where
encouragement (*paraklēsis*) and incentive (*paramythion*) are also
used in conjunction with one another, is unmistakable. The
parallelism in meaning between these two terms makes it clear

---

[1] Col 4:16 (And when this letter has been read among you, have it read also in the
church of the Laodiceans; and see that you read also the letter from Laodicea).

that the phrase "encouragement in Christ, any incentive of love" should be understood, as is the case in 1 Corinthians, as a request to preach and teach the love for the neighbor within the church of Philippi as the "rule (law) of the messiah" (*nomos Khristou*; Gal 6:2). This is corroborated in the following phrase "participation (*koinōnia*) in the Spirit, affection (entrails; *splankhna*) and sympathy (compassions, mercies; *oiktirmoi*)." In Galatians, the messianic law of love is implemented through the authoritative agency of God's spirit (5:13-16) who ensures the *koinōnia*, the fellowship between the believers based on their partnership in the gospel, which in turn is basically love for the neighbor expressed at table fellowship (Gal 2:11-14; 1 Cor 10:16-21) and an attitude reflecting genuine[2] mercy and compassion toward the others (Gal 5:22-23; 6:1-3). This in turn is corroborated in a passage of Colossians:

> Put to death therefore what is earthly in you: fornication, impurity, passion, evil desire, and covetousness, which is idolatry. On account of these the wrath of God is coming. In these you once walked, when you lived in them. But now put them all away: anger, wrath, malice, slander, and foul talk from your mouth. Do not lie to one another, seeing that you have put off the old nature with its practices and have put on the new nature, which is being renewed in knowledge after the image of its creator. Here there cannot be Greek and Jew, circumcised and uncircumcised, barbarian, Scythian, slave, free man, but Christ is all, and in all. Put on then, as God's chosen ones, holy and beloved, compassion (entrails of compassion; *splankhna oiktirmou*), kindness, lowliness (*tapeinophrosynēn*), meekness, and patience, forbearing one another and, if one has a complaint against another, forgiving each other; as the Lord has forgiven you, so you also must forgive. And

---

[2] Coming from one's entrails, that is, the womb, seat of one's inner feelings.

above all these put on love, which binds everything together in
perfect harmony. And let the peace of Christ rule in your hearts,
to which indeed you were called in the one body. And be
thankful. Let the word of Christ dwell in you richly, admonish
(*nouthetountes*) and teach one another in all wisdom, and sing
psalms and hymns and spiritual songs with thankfulness in your
hearts to God. (3:5-16)

This passage is clearly patterned after Galatians 5 where the
condemnable desires of the flesh will undergo God's wrath, and
God's will is expressed in the love for the neighbor through
kindness (*khrēstotēta*; Col 3:12; Gal 5:22), meekness (*prautēta*;
Col 3:12; Gal 5:23; 6:1), and patience (*makrothymia*; Col 3:12;
Gal 5:22). The link to Philippians is evidenced through the
following features: (1) the use of "entrails of compassion"; (2) the
link of this phrase to love; (3) the "word of Christ," that is, the
law of Christ will teach and admonish (*nouthetountes*) the
believers;[3] (4) Christ himself is given as an example to follow; (5)
this example is subsumed in the term *tapeinophrosynēn*, which
qualifies Christ's behavior (Phil 2:8) and is required from the
Philippians (2:3).

Starting with Philippians 2:1, Paul smoothly prepares for his
second move: setting Christ, beyond himself, as the example for
the Philippians to follow. He does so through the use of
"entrails" (*splankhna*) which he already introduced in speaking of
his relationship to them: "For God is my witness, how I yearn
for you all with the affection (*en splankhnois*) of Christ Jesus."

---

[3] The root *nouthet—* is parallel in meaning with the root *paramyth—* as can be seen
from Paul's request of the Thessalonians: "And we exhort you, brethren, admonish
(*noutheteite*) the idlers, encourage (*paramytheisthe*) the fainthearted, help the weak, be
patient with them all." (1 Thess 5:14)

(1:8) However, the example set by Christ is not to be viewed differently from that of Paul himself; they are both equivalent as can be gathered from the same vocabulary used to speak of both:

> Only let your manner of life be worthy of the gospel of Christ, so that whether I come and see you or am absent, I may hear of you that you stand firm in *one spirit* (*eni pnevmati*), with *one mind* (one soul; *mia psykhē*) striving side by side for the faith of the gospel ... engaged in *the same* (*ton avton*) conflict which you saw and now hear to be mine. (1:27, 30).

> So if there is any encouragement in Christ, any incentive of love, any participation in the *Spirit* (*pnevmatos*), any affection and sympathy, complete my joy by being of *the same mind* (thinking *the same* thing; *to avto phronēte*), having *the same* (*tēn avtēn*) love, being in full accord (of one soul; *sympsykhoi*)[4] and of *one* mind (thinking the *one* thing; *to en phronountes*). (2:1-2)

However, contrary to what is usually assumed, full and total "oneness" will never be attained by applying the rule of equality; rather it can only be realized whenever one comes from "below" in one's relationship with the others. As early as Galatians Paul set down this ruling: "For you were called to freedom, brethren; only do not use your freedom as an opportunity for the flesh, but through love be servants of (*doulevete*; be enslaved to) one another." (5:13) Here, in Philippians, he elaborated on the "how" by using a terminology that makes Christ and Paul the prime examples of such an attitude: although they were actually superior to all those around them, they nonetheless both behaved as inferiors.

---

[4] The preposition *syn* in *sympsykhoi* (of one soul) corresponds to that found in the verb *synathlountes* (striving side by side) that is qualified by "with one soul" in 1:27.

Paul already made it clear in chapter 1 that he did "count" the Philippians of better or higher value than he by putting their need above his preference (Phil 1:23-26) and thus "putting their interests over his own." Now he is requiring them in turn to do this to others (2:4). In so doing they will eschew "selfish ambition (partisanship)" (*eritheian* 3:5) just as he himself did (*eritheias*; 1:17). After having given as examples Christ, their superior, and Timothy, their counterpart in that both he and they are Paul's children,[5] Paul will revert to his own example in chapter 3. He prepares for that later passage by using here terminology he will pick up when speaking of himself. In the same phrase in which he uses the key word "humility" (2:3) that prepares for speaking of Christ (he humbled himself; v.8) as an example for the Philippians to follow, Paul uses two terms that will reappear later when speaking of himself:

> ... but in humility *count* others *better* (*hyperekhontas*) than yourselves. (2:5)

> But whatever gain I had, I *counted* as loss for the sake of Christ. Indeed I *count* everything as loss because of the *surpassing worth* (*hyperekhon*) of knowing Christ Jesus my Lord. For his sake I have suffered the loss of all things, and *count* them as refuse, in order that I may gain Christ. (3:7-8)

The intentional link between these two passages is further evidenced in that, in the latter instance, we find the terminology

---

[5] See also 1 Cor 4:14-17: "I do not write this to make you ashamed, but to admonish you as my beloved children. For though you have countless guides in Christ, you do not have many fathers. For I became your father in Christ Jesus through the gospel. I urge you, then, be imitators of me. Therefore I sent to you Timothy, my beloved and faithful child in the Lord, to remind you of my ways in Christ, as I teach them everywhere in every church."

used in chapter 1 where Paul describes his behavior toward the Philippians: "For to me to live is Christ, and to die is gain." (1:21) By losing his own life for Christ's gospel for the sake of the Philippians' need, Paul actually ends up ensured of gaining it! And this is precisely what Christ is presented as having done, for by putting in jeopardy what he has for the sake of others, out of obedience to God's will, he actually gained for himself God's goodwill in a "superlative" way: "God has *superlatively*[6] exalted him." (2:9)

Two features give unequivocal confirmation of Paul's intent to present Christ and himself as intertwined and as concomitant examples for the Philippians. The first is the verb "count," which functions as the primary link between the behaviors of the three. Besides its centrality in the case of Paul and the Philippians, as mentioned above, it is the first active indicative verb in the description of Jesus' actions: "who, though he was in the form of God, did not count equality with God a thing to be grasped" (2:6) Further, Paul uses the same terminology both to introduce Christ's paradigm and to conclude his own:

> Let each of you look (*skopountes*) not only to his own interests, but also to the interests of others. Have this mind (*phroneite*) among yourselves, which is yours in Christ Jesus. (2:4-5)

> I press on toward the goal (*skopon*) for the prize of the upward call of God in Christ Jesus. Let those of us who are mature be thus minded (*phronōmen*); and if in anything you are otherwise minded (*phroneite*), God will reveal that also to you. Only let us hold true to what we have attained. Brethren, join in imitating me, and

---

[6] The Greek verb *hyperypsōsen* has the same preposition *hyper* found in *hyperekhontas* (2:5) and *hyperekhon* (3:7).

mark (*skopeite*) those who so live as you have an example in us. (3:14-17)

Vv. 6-11 ⁶ὃς ἐν μορφῇ θεοῦ ὑπάρχων οὐχ ἁρπαγμὸν ἡγήσατο τὸ εἶναι ἴσα θεῷ, ⁷ἀλλὰ ἑαυτὸν ἐκένωσεν μορφὴν δούλου λαβών, ἐν ὁμοιώματι ἀνθρώπων γενόμενος· καὶ σχήματι εὑρεθεὶς ὡς ἄνθρωπος ⁸ἐταπείνωσεν ἑαυτὸν γενόμενος ὑπήκοος μέχρι θανάτου, θανάτου δὲ σταυροῦ. ⁹διὸ καὶ ὁ θεὸς αὐτὸν ὑπερύψωσεν καὶ ἐχαρίσατο αὐτῷ τὸ ὄνομα τὸ ὑπὲρ πᾶν ὄνομα, ¹⁰ἵνα ἐν τῷ ὀνόματι Ἰησοῦ πᾶν γόνυ κάμψῃ ἐπουρανίων καὶ ἐπιγείων καὶ καταχθονίων ¹¹καὶ πᾶσα γλῶσσα ἐξομολογήσηται ὅτι κύριος Ἰησοῦς Χριστὸς εἰς δόξαν θεοῦ πατρός.

> ⁶*who, though he was in the form of God, did not count equality with God a thing to be grasped,* ⁷*but emptied himself, taking the form of a servant, being born in the likeness of men.* ⁸*And being found in human form he humbled himself and became obedient unto death, even death on a cross.* ⁹*Therefore God has highly exalted him and bestowed on him the name which is above every name,* ¹⁰*that at the name of Jesus every knee should bow, in heaven and on earth and under the earth,* ¹¹*and every tongue confess that Jesus Christ is Lord, to the glory of God the Father.*

As the previous discussion confirmed, the appeal to the person of Jesus Christ at this juncture is to present him as the *example of behavior* to be followed by the Philippians *in the same vein as Paul* and eventually Timothy. This clearly being the case, it becomes painful, to say the least, to witness the fate of this "hymn" at the hand of "theologians" who excised it out of its context and made out of it a self-standing source for theologico-philosophical pontifications à la Plato and Plotinus on the "person" of Christ after the manner of the school of Alexandria that exercised undue influence on subsequent "dogmatic theology."[7] The passage's terminology and content are so enmeshed with the rest of the epistle that it stands to reason to conclude that Philippians 2:5-11 is not a self-standing hymn in honor of Jesus Christ, that was circulating independently of the epistle and which the author "threw in" at this juncture because somehow it speaks of Christ's humility. The outcome of such a presupposition is to deal with the hymn as a piece on its own, independent of the epistle.[8] Unfortunately this is what is often done even in commentaries on the epistle.

Just as was the case with Galatians 4:1-7, the "hymn" (Phil 2:6-11) is an integral part of the epistle and the work of the epistle's author in conjunction with his writing to the Philippians. It is then only the argumentation and the line of thought of the entire epistle which will reveal to us the "function" of the passage within the epistle's argument and thus will shed light on its meaning. The "hymn," just as the rest of the epistle, does not speak of an imaginary, self-standing Christ,

---

[7] I shall not engage here into a fruitless debate with such a blatant eisegetical methodology. I have dealt extensively with a similar passage (Gal 4:1-7) where I showed that it spoke of Christ functionally as God's *emissary* rather than on the level of essence and pre-existence and I should like to refer my readers to that discussion in *Gal* 201-206.

[8] Witness to this are volumes such as Ralph P. Martin, *A Hymn of Christ: Philippians 2:5-11 in Recent Interpretation & in the Setting of Early Christian Worship* (Downers Grove, IL: InterVarsity Press) issued in 1983 and then revisited fifteen years later in 1997. At the end of the 1997 preface Martin writes: "Given that this new preface marks a milestone in a series of publications that go back to 1959, some may view *devoting some forty years to a study of a six-verse biblical passage* as a tedious and exacting chore. Yet, it has been a task lightened by ... above all, the chance to *penetrate the mind of whoever wrote the hymn*, the experience of those who sang, heard or were challenged by it, and the wisdom of *the apostle who recorded it* (italics mine)."

but rather the Pauline Christ who—unlike the "other false Christs" (2 Cor 11:4; see also Mt 24:24/Mk 13:22)—"comes to us" *out of the* epistle's *total text,* or at least in the immediate context, as it structurally stands and in the sequence in which it stands.

For the sake of brevity, let me concentrate on the immediate context. After having spoken extensively of his apostolate and its costs, Paul ends by giving himself as the example for the Philippians to follow (1:30). He does so by asking them in v.27 to proceed on the way they started, whether he is present or absent, and does so in terminology similar to what he uses to open chapter 2.[9] Immediately after the Christological passage he iterates his request to the Philippians that they continue the labor they had started "not only as in my presence but much more in my absence" (2:12). Thus, clearly Paul is simply repeating the same request in order to underline that, in following his behavior, the Philippians are actually following in the footsteps of their common Lord. In other words, Paul is telling them they ought to follow his behavior in the same way that he, whom they know, follows in the footsteps of Christ, whom they have never known except through Paul. This Pauline approach, linking his addressees to Christ through himself, is a trademark of his writings: "... to those sanctified in Christ Jesus, called to be saints together with all those who in every place call on the name of our Lord Jesus Christ, both their Lord and ours" (1 Cor 1:2); "For I became your father in Christ Jesus through the gospel. I urge you, then, be imitators of me" (4:15-16); "Be

---

[9] See my comments earlier.

imitators of me, as I am of Christ" (11:1); "And you became imitators of us and of the Lord" (1 Thess 1:6). That the imitation of Paul is the primary invitation will be confirmed later in the epistle: "Brethren, join in imitating me, and mark those who so live as you have an example in us." (Phil 3:17)

The conclusion is inescapable. Christ is brought into the picture only secondarily to underscore Paul's request. The "artificiality" of the parenthesis concerning Christ is detectable in that the three indicative verbs—*hēgēsato*, count, v.6; *ekenōsen*, emptied, v.7; *etapeinōsen*, humbled, v.8— describing Jesus Christ's "behavior" correspond to the terminology of Philippians 2:3—*kenodoxian*, vain [empty] glory; *tapeinophrosynē*, humility; *hēgoumenoi*, counting—, thus betraying the author's intention that the addressees, slaves as are Paul and Timothy (1:1), have no excuse but to follow the example of these two. After all, the Philippians have never seen Christ; they only heard of him from these two. However, if the Lord himself (1:2) behaved in full obedience as a slave would (2:7), it is not too much to ask "his slaves" Paul and Timothy (1:2) and their disciples in Philippi to do the same. When it comes to Christ, it is his "obedience until death" that is highlighted as his main feature (2:8), the reason being that it is precisely this quality which will be required of the Philippians in the conclusion drawn from the Christological passage: "Therefore, my beloved, as you have always obeyed, so now, not only as in my presence but much more in my absence, work out your own salvation with fear and trembling." (v.12) They were already obeying, but Paul is using the example of Christ to ask them to continue doing so "until their last breath" and not to take the opportunity of Paul's "absence"—that is, his eventual death—to cease their obedience to the gospel teaching.

The "artificiality" of the passage is at its clearest when one considers its content. It is not in the least pre-Pauline or non-Pauline, let alone "theological," as it is customarily assumed. Rather it is conceived and formulated along pure Pauline lines: it both presents Christ "according to the scriptures" and underscores the shame element connected with his crucifixion, which are *the* Pauline trademarks beginning with the Apostle's earliest epistle, his letter to the churches of Galatia, and which trademarks were imposed by his school on the rest of the New Testament literature.[10] The classical Old Testament texts describing a person that is the epitome of total and absolute obedience are the Isaianic passages of the Lord's Servant (Is 42:1-5; 49:1-4; 50:5-8; 52:13-53:12). The noun servant is the translation of the Hebrew *'ebed* and its counterpart the Greek *doulos*, both meaning "slave."[11] One cannot but conclude that Philippians 2:6-11, whose first part revolves around Christ as "obedient slave," originated in Isaiah's passages. The link to Second-Isaiah (Is 40-55) is confirmed through a quotation from that prophet at the end of the Philippians passage:

> By myself I have sworn, from my mouth has gone forth in righteousness a word that shall not return: "To me every knee shall bow (*kampsei pan gony*), every tongue shall swear (*kai exomologēsetai pasa glōssa tō theō*)." (Is 45:23 LXX)

---

[10] See my 4 volumes of *New Testament Introduction: NTI₁, NTI₂, NTI₃, NTI₄*.

[11] The importance, if not centrality, of these Isaianic passages is evident in their ubiquitous presence in the New Testament books.

... that at the name of Jesus every knee should *kampsē*), in heaven and on earth and under the tongue confess (*kai pasa glōssa exomologēsetai*) that Jesus Lord, to the glory of God (*theou*) the Father. (Phil 2:10-11)

Given the restrictions imposed by the size of parchments, quoting a verse or two from the Old Testament functions as an invitation for the hearers to refer to an entire section of a book and the teaching of that section.[12]

The question is then, "What is the main thesis of Second-Isaiah and how was it used in Philippians?" Isaiah was dubbed "the fifth evangelist" in early Christian tradition mainly because of his extensive use of the verb "evangelize" (*evangelizomai*, whence *evangelion* [gospel]) in chapters 40-66. Another reason is the affluence of "messianic prophecies" and the main title of the main personage in the New Testament, Jesus (whose Hebrew name is from the same root as Isaiah), is the "Messiah" (Christ). However, a closer look at the entire Book of Isaiah will reveal that its central interest is God's heavenly city, Zion, where the new David will reign, as a counterpart to Jerusalem, the unfaithful city of (the first) David, to the extent that one can refer to the Book of Isaiah as "the story of God with his city."[13] Indeed, the headings of both the introductory chapter to the entire book and chapter 2 that opens the story betray this concern: "The vision of Isaiah the son of Amoz, which he saw concerning Judah and Jerusalem in the days of Uzziah, Jotham, Ahaz, and Hezekiah, kings of Judah" (1:1); "The word which

---

[12] As I explained in the case of Galatians 4:26-27 in *Gal* 249-250.
[13] See *OTI₂* 197-98.

saiah the son of Amoz saw concerning Judah and Jerusalem." (2:1) Moreover, not only does the introductory chapter deal with the unfaithfulness of Jerusalem and announces its restoration, but each of the following three parts (2-39; 40-55; 56-66) are woven around the tension between the sinful city and the heavenly Zion:

1. The first part (Is 2-39) opens up with a description of God's heavenly city where the Lord's teaching in his law is the light guiding both Israel and the nations (2:2-4). Although Israel is asked to walk in this light (v.5), it nevertheless falters (vv.6-22). The rest (chs.3-39) is a detailed description of Israel's and the nations' disobedience, culminating with a prediction of Jerusalem's total punishment (ch.39).

2. The second part (Is 40-55) starts with the gospel message to Zion after it had paid double for its sins: "Comfort, comfort my people, says your God. Speak tenderly to Jerusalem, and cry to her that her warfare is ended, that her iniquity is pardoned, that she has received from the Lord's hand double for all her sins ... Get you up to a high mountain, O Zion, *herald of good tidings* (*evangelizomenos*); lift up your voice with strength, O Jerusalem, *herald of good tidings* (*evangelizomenos*), lift it up, fear not; say to the cities of Judah, 'Behold your God!'" (40:1-2, 9) It ends with a description of God's city (54:10-17) under the aegis of the new David who will enlighten both Israel and the nations with God's teaching (55:1-7).

3.   The third part is an *inclusio*: it both starts and ends with an address to God's new city that will house both Israel and the nations within its walls (56:1-7; 66:17-24).

In the second part, which is more specifically the "gospel" section, we encounter the four passages of the Suffering Servant who is the divine emissary to and implementer of God's law among the nations as well as within Israel (Is 42:6-7; 49:6). Not only is his total and absolute obedience to God underscored, but also at the end of each of the hymns we find an ode to God's heavenly city (Is 42:10-17; 49:13-26; 51:1-52:12; 54) heralding that this city is brought about through the intermediacy of that Servant. This teaching was at the heart of Paul's gospel early on, as is clear from Galatians 4:21-28.[14] The letter to the Philippians follows this lead. Whereas Galatians speaks in terms of "children of the Jerusalem above," Philippians, addressed to the mini-Rome Philippi, uses the terminology of "citizenry in the heavenly city." It stands to reason then, that the writer would show the person of Isaiah's Suffering Servant as the top example for "citizens" who are asked to continue in their obedience to the "law of the land" (Phil 2:13), so to speak. As this "slave" was raised in glory by the God whom he obeyed, so will the other "citizens" join him in that glory upon his "coming" (3:20-21). This teaching is thoroughly Pauline, as is evident from Romans 6 and 1 Corinthians 15. Indeed, just as the Philippians text pointing out the parallelism between Christ and the believers concludes with an invitation to obedience (Phil 2:1-13), the passage on baptism underscoring the parallelism between the

---

[14] See my comments in *Gal* 245-46.

same in their "dying" (Rom 6:1-11) concludes with an exhortation to "obedient slavery":

> Let not sin therefore reign in your mortal bodies, to make you obey their passions. Do not yield your members to sin as instruments of wickedness, but yield yourselves to God as men who have been brought from death to life, and your members to God as instruments of righteousness. For sin will have no dominion over you, since you are not under law but under grace. What then? Are we tó sin because we are not under law but under grace? By no means! Do you not know that if you yield yourselves to any one as obedient slaves, you are slaves of the one whom you obey, either of sin, which leads to death, or of obedience, which leads to righteousness? But thanks be to God, that you who were once slaves of sin have become obedient from the heart to the standard of teaching to which you were committed, and, having been set free from sin, have become slaves of righteousness. I am speaking in human terms, because of your natural limitations. For just as you once yielded your members to impurity and to greater and greater iniquity, so now yield your members to righteousness for sanctification. When you were slaves of sin, you were free in regard to righteousness. But then what return did you get from the things of which you are now ashamed? The end of those things is death. But now that you have been set free from sin and have become slaves of God, the return you get is sanctification and its end, eternal life. For the wages of sin is death, but the free gift of God is eternal life in Christ Jesus our Lord. (Rom 6:12-23)

We find the same teaching in 1 Corinthians 15. In order to join Christ in his victory over death, the last enemy that is still ahead (vv.20-29, 54-55, 57) and is the result of sin (v.56), Paul concludes by urging his hearers thus: "Therefore, my beloved brethren, be steadfast, immovable, always abounding in the work

of the Lord, knowing that in the Lord your labor is not in vain."
(v.58)

One can find further evidence for the last hymn of the
Suffering Servant (Is 52:12-53:12) being the source for
Philippians 2:6-11 in that the terminology of exaltation and
glory with which it ends (Phil 2:9, 11) is precisely the main
point of the Isaianic hymn: "Behold my servant will understand
and will be exalted and glorified exceedingly." (Is 52:13 LXX)
Then Isaiah proceeds to show that the path toward this exalted
status is bound to the Servant's obedience, which is precisely the
thesis of the Philippians passage. At no point in handling the
"mission" of the obedient Jesus in Galatians, Romans, and 1
Corinthians does one detect the idea of pre-existence.[15] How
does one explain that the terminology of the first part of the
Philippians Christological passage seems to point to "pre-
existence"? The clauses around the indicative verbs "emptied
himself" and "humbled himself" (Phil 2:7-8) on their own do
not account for such an impression. It is only the statement
"though being in the form of God, he did not count equality
with God a thing to be held to" (v.6) that bears the entire
burden. Given the rest of the Pauline literature, one should look
for other plausible explanations before jumping the gun and
endorsing the eisegetical readings of later theology. How then is
one to understand that verse in context?

First and foremost, the "but" (*alla*) at the beginning of v.7
invites us to take the (grammatically) positive actions of the
emptying and the humbling as parallel to the (grammatically)

---

[15] See my comments on Gal 4:4-5 in *Gal* 201-206.

negative action of "not counting." Thus, the unexpected behavior starts with the "not counting one's equality with God a matter to be clung to." That is to say, the entire passage vv.6b-8 is to be read as an unlikely conduct for someone who is "in the form of God." When read in context, this phrase does not lend itself to philosophico-theological constructions about a "pre-existent person or personality." It is rather to be read in function of both the following verses and the entire epistle. The term *morphē* (form) ensures actually the link between the three parallel statements in vv.6, 7, and 8: it is used again in v.7 and its synonym *skhēma* (shape, appearance; translated as "form" in RSV) occurs in v.8. There is no reason to differentiate between the meanings of these two terms since they are used as parallels later in the epistle: "who will change (*metaskhēmatisei*) our lowly body to be like (*symmorphon*) his glorious body, by the power which enables him even to subject all things to himself." (3:21) In 2:7-8, the "form" does not reflect any ontological quality; rather it is linked to conduct, which actually fits the context where Paul is asking the Philippians to behave in a certain way. This is actually confirmed in the parallel passage in Romans 12 where the Apostle's behest is concerning the behavior required of his hearers and where we encounter the same terminology found in Philippians 2:

> Do not be conformed (*syskhēmatizesthe*) to this world but be transformed (*metamorphousthe*) by the renewal of your mind, that you may prove what is the will of God, what is good and acceptable and perfect. For by the grace given to me I bid every one among you not to think of himself more highly (*hyperphronein*) than he ought to think (*phronein*) ... Let *love* be genuine ... love one another with brotherly affection; outdo

(*proēgoumenoi*) one another in showing honor … Live
(*phronountes*) in harmony (*to avto*) with one another; do not be
haughty (*ta hypsēla*[16] *phronountes*), but associate with the lowly
(*tois tapeinois*); never be conceited. (Rom 12:2-3, 9-10, 16)[17]

The conclusion imposes itself. The first instance of "form"
(Phil 2:6) must be related to an expected behavior, one that
would befit someone who is "equal to a deity" and thus a "lord"
and not "in the likeness of human beings," who are servants of
the deity, their lord. The only lordship of Jesus that both Paul
and the Philippians are privy to is the lordship bestowed upon
Jesus by God at God's raising him from the dead:

> Paul, a servant of Jesus Christ, called to be an apostle, set apart
> (*aphōrismenos*) for the gospel of God which he promised
> beforehand through his prophets in the holy scriptures, the gospel
> concerning his Son, who was descended from David according to
> the flesh and designated (*horisthentos*) Son of God in power
> according to the Spirit of holiness by his resurrection from the
> dead, Jesus Christ our Lord, through whom we have received
> grace and apostleship to bring about the obedience of faith for the
> sake of his name among all the nations, including yourselves who
> are called to belong to Jesus Christ; To all God's beloved in Rome,
> who are called to be saints: Grace to you and peace from God our
> Father and the Lord Jesus Christ. (Rom 1:1-7)

As the two original verbs indicate, Paul's apostleship to the
nations is intimately connected to God's raising Jesus from the
domain of the dead. This is precisely what Paul already stated in
Galatians, the precursor to the letter to the Romans:

---

[16] The opposite of "lowly" (*tapeina*).

[17] The phrase "*renewal* of your mind" recalls "so that … we too might walk in *newness*
of life" (Rom 6:4) in a passage dealing with the behavior expected of the believer and
which I showed to have the same thought as Phil 2:1-13.

Paul an apostle—not from men nor through man, but through
Jesus Christ and God the Father, who raised him from the dead
... For I would have you know, brethren, that the gospel which
was preached by me is not man's gospel. For I did not receive it
from man, nor was I taught it, but it came through a revelation
concerning Jesus Christ... But when he who had set me apart
before I was born, and had called me through his grace, was
pleased to reveal his Son to me, in order that I might preach him
among the Gentiles, I did not confer with flesh and blood, nor did
I go up to Jerusalem to those who were apostles before me, but I
went away into Arabia. (Gal 1:1, 11-12, 15-17)

The corollary is that the Philippians' perception of Jesus'
lordship through his having been raised by God from the dead
cannot be but indirect, bound by whatever Paul said to them:

Now if Christ *is preached as* raised from the dead, how can some of
you say that there is no resurrection of the dead? But if there is no
resurrection of the dead, then Christ has not been raised; if Christ
has not been raised, then *our preaching is in vain and your faith is
in vain.* We are even found to be misrepresenting God, because we
testified of God that he raised Christ, whom he did not raise if it is
true that the dead are not raised. For if the dead are not raised,
then Christ has not been raised. If Christ has not been raised, *your
faith is futile and you are still in your sins.* (1 Cor 15:12-17)

Contrary to the widespread assumption—that it is Christ's
raising that is the basis for the coming resurrection of all from
the dead—it is rather the latter which is the basis of the former:
it is *because* there is "in accordance with the scriptures" (v.4) a
resurrection from the dead (Dan 12:2) that the raising of Christ
is "scripturally speaking" a given. However, that he was *already*
raised is *communicated* to the Corinthians and all other Gentiles
by Paul in order to prepare them for God's judgment that will

decide whether their raising will be unto life or death (Dan 12:2). Indeed, the resurrected Christ "died for our sins in accordance with the scriptures" (1 Cor 15:3), that is, in accordance with Isaiah 53, and it is up to the Corinthians to put their trust in this Paul's teaching or remain "in their sins" (1 Cor 15:17) and succumb to God's judgment that will be done "according to my [Paul's] gospel" (Rom 2:16). This is precisely what we are faced with in the conclusion (Phil 2:12-13) to the Christological passage (vv.6-11).

Thus, as is clear from Jesus' earliest call in the Gospels, the "gospel news" is not information *about* Jesus and his person; it is rather an invitation to change one's ways in view of the coming kingdom: "Now after John was arrested, Jesus came into Galilee, preaching the gospel of God, and saying, 'The time is fulfilled, and the kingdom of God is at hand; *repent* and believe (trust in) the gospel.'" (Mk 1:14-15) One is to assume that Matthew understood Mark correctly when he allowed for his expanded version:

> Now when he heard that John had been arrested, he withdrew into Galilee; and leaving Nazareth he went and dwelt in Capernaum by the sea, in the territory of Zebulun and Naphtali, that what was spoken by the prophet Isaiah might be fulfilled: "The land of Zebulun and the land of Naphtali, toward the sea, across the Jordan, Galilee of the Gentiles—the people who sat in darkness have seen a great light, and for those who sat in the region and shadow of death light has dawned." From that time Jesus began to preach, saying, "*Repent*, for the kingdom of heaven is at hand." (Mt 4:12-17)

Besides putting in relief the call to repentance, Matthew appeals to Isaiah, the prophet shown to be the source behind the Christological passage of Philippians. What is more interesting is that he quotes a passage where reference is made both to the Gentiles, among whom the Philippians were, and to the message as being a "light." Both metaphors are taken up in the "hymns" of the Suffering Servant: "I am the Lord, I have called you in righteousness, I have taken you by the hand and kept you; I have given you as a covenant to the people, a light to the nations, to open the eyes that are blind, to bring out the prisoners from the dungeon, from the prison those who sit in darkness" (Is 42:6-7); "It is too light a thing that you should be my servant to raise up the tribes of Jacob and to restore the preserved of Israel; I will give you as a light to the nations, that my salvation may reach to the end of the earth" (49:6). In Isaiah, this light is none other than that dispensed in God's law:

> It shall come to pass in the latter days that the mountain of the house of the Lord shall be established as the highest of the mountains, and shall be raised above the hills; and all the nations shall flow to it, and many peoples shall come, and say: "Come, let us go up to the mountain of the Lord, to the house of the God of Jacob; that he may teach us his ways and that we may walk in his paths." For out of Zion shall go forth the law, and the word of the Lord from Jerusalem. He shall judge between the nations, and shall decide for many peoples; and they shall beat their swords into plowshares, and their spears into pruning hooks; nation shall not lift up sword against nation, neither shall they learn war any more. O house of Jacob, come, let us walk in the light of the Lord. (2:2-5)

> Behold my servant, whom I uphold, my chosen, in whom my soul delights; I have put my Spirit upon him, he will bring forth justice

to the nations. He will not cry or lift up his voice, or make it heard in the street; a bruised reed he will not break, and a dimly burning wick he will not quench; he will faithfully bring forth justice. He will not fail or be discouraged till he has established justice in the earth; and the coastlands wait for his law. (42:1-4)

Listen to me, my people, and give ear to me, my nation; for a law will go forth from me, and my justice for a light to the peoples. My deliverance draws near speedily, my salvation has gone forth, and my arms will rule the peoples; the coastlands wait for me, and for my arm they hope. (51:4-5)

If we look at Philippians from this scriptural angle, then the function of the Christological passage becomes clear: to invite the Philippians to follow "the law of Christ" (Gal 6:2). After all, Paul never met Jesus Christ except raised from the dead, that is, as the Lord who commissioned him to *do* something (1 Cor 9:1; 15:8; Acts 9:1-9; 22:6-11; 26:12-18).[18] Lordship here is not a theoretical, theological issue to be debated. Rather, a lord gives orders to be followed, and his orders to Paul, his slave (Rom 1:1), are clear: make the nations submit obediently to God's will (Rom 1:5) so that they in turn become his slaves and, in so doing, acquiesce that he is their Lord also: "To the church of God which is at Corinth, to those sanctified in Christ Jesus, called to be saints together with all those who in every place call on the name of our Lord Jesus Christ, *both their Lord and ours*." (1 Cor 1:2) How did Paul arrive at this conclusion?

Even a casual reader of Paul's epistles cannot help but notice the centrality of the cross and the crucifixion in his thought. In

---

[18] As for the Philippians, they did not even see Christ; they only were preached that he was the Lord.

Galatians, his first letter, this feature is unmistakable since it brackets his argumentation:

> I have been crucified with Christ; it is no longer I who live, but Christ who lives in me; and the life I now live in the flesh I live by faith in the Son of God, who loved me and gave himself for me. I do not nullify the grace of God; for if justification were through the law, then Christ died to no purpose. O foolish Galatians! Who has bewitched you, before whose eyes Jesus Christ was publicly portrayed as crucified? (2:20-3:1)

> It is those who want to make a good showing in the flesh that would compel you to be circumcised, and only in order that they may not be persecuted for the cross of Christ. For even those who receive circumcision do not themselves keep the law, but they desire to have you circumcised that they may boast in your flesh. But far be it from me to boast except in the cross of our Lord Jesus Christ, by which the world has been crucified to me, and I to the world. (6:12-14)

Thereafter, "cross" or "crucified" is found in each of Romans, 1 Corinthians, 2 Corinthians, Ephesians, Philippians, and Colossians. In 1 Corinthians, we have a text where the "cross" is squarely equated with the content of the gospel itself:

> For Christ did not send me to baptize but to evangelize (*evangelizesthai*), and not with eloquent wisdom, lest the cross of Christ be *emptied*. For the word (*ho logos*), namely the one referring to the cross (*ho tou stavrou*), is folly to those who are perishing, but to us who are being saved it is the power of God. (1:17-18)

If the cross can be emptied, it is because it has content. And the reason is clear: Paul is evangelizing "the word," which is another term he uses to refer to the gospel he is preaching. This is further confirmed in that, in Romans, Paul speaks of the gospel as being the power of God (1:17). However, in this case he prefaces his statement by saying that he is not ashamed of the gospel. Such shame is the opposite of boasting. So, here again, we see indirectly that the cross he is boasting of in Galatians is, in a nutshell, the gospel he is not ashamed of in Romans. The clue to making sense out of this factual equation between "gospel" and "cross" lies in the aspect of shameful death linked to the cross in the Roman Empire. Crucifixion was intended for public humiliation and was the punishment administered to slaves, foreigners, and those involved in a revolt against the legal authority. It was the opposite of the soldier's glorious death for the sake of a noble cause: martyrdom for one's own country or nation or empire. Crucifixion was a death unto total oblivion of someone whose life was unworthy of remembrance: an unworthy end of an unworthy life, shame ending in shame.

This is precisely what Paul found in Isaiah 52:13-53:12: an *incredible* story. God's chosen one, his "slave," is raised from an unimpressive death, that of a slaughtered lamb, into a position of power that surpasses that of mighty kings. Moreover, God's new city, polity, to which all are invited—the nations as well as Israel—is the outcome of such a story. Put otherwise, God chose to build his kingdom in this implausible way: "Who has believed what we have heard? And to whom has the arm of the Lord been revealed?" (Is 53:1) On the other hand, this inconceivable news is repeatedly said to be announced through "evangelization" to both the scattered sheep of Israel and the nations.[19] It is thus Isaiah's "scripture" that defined Paul's mission: he would evangelize to the nations—while his colleague Peter would evangelize to the Jewish diaspora—the *one* gospel of God (Gal 2:7-8)[20] as "promised beforehand" and consigned "through his prophets in the holy scriptures" (Rom 1:2). That, in Philippians, the writer is following Isaiah's story line which stressed the shameful death, can be seen in the unnecessary addition "even death on the cross" (Phil 2:8) at the end of the passage describing the unexpected behavior of the one "in the form of God and equal to him."

It is worth noting here that this aspect of a shameful death was glossed over, if not totally lost, in classical theology which spoke of the scandal linked to the "death of Christ *as God*." The closest theology comes to the original meaning of crucifixion is to speak of it as a death with extra suffering, which still misses the mark and gives rise only to feelings of sorrow and empathy without any real challenge to accept utter shame for the sake of the crucified Son of man (Mt 16:24-28/Mk 8:24-9:1/Lk 9:23-27). When reading theological treatises dealing with the cross, one finds a plain equation between it and death: death on the cross and death are equivalent. Notice for instance the full equivalence in theological idiom between "the cross (crucifixion) and resurrection of Christ" and "the death and resurrection of Christ."

---

[19] The content of the Servant's "gospel" to the captives among the children of Israel (Is 61:1) is the same as the one he is mandated to carry also to the nations (42:6-7).

[20] See my comments on Gal 2:7-8 regarding the one gospel and the one apostolic mission in *Gal* 69-70.

Classical theology, under the influence of philosophy, introduced the notion of "pre-existence" over and above "mission" when dealing with the "sending" of Christ, and also referred to the "pre-ordained" message of God as being "eternal." However, in Second-Isaiah, the "gospel" message is said to have been there from the beginning, meaning that God had uttered it through his prophet Isaiah (Is 2-39) well before the rise, and thus existence, of the Chaldeans as a world power on the historical scene. Even more, God had foreordained through the same Isaiah that God himself would punish Jerusalem at the hand of the Chaldeans, these being merely his agents as the Assyrians were when he punished Samaria. The important point is that God's statements concerning the situation at hand were uttered *before* that situation arose. It is in the same vein that Paul refers to his gospel message as being "before the ages." His Isaianic approach to the matter is corroborated in a passage in 1 Corinthians where he refers to that prophet in such conjunction:

> But we impart a secret and hidden wisdom of God, which God decreed before the ages for our glorification. None of the rulers of this age understood this; for if they had, they would not have crucified the Lord of glory. But, as it is written, "What no eye has seen, nor ear heard, nor the heart of man conceived, what God has prepared for those who love him." (1 Cor 2:7-9)

Such is only expected from someone who viewed God's "eternal" gospel[21] as "promised beforehand through his prophets in the

---

[21] See Eph 3:7-12: "Of this gospel I was made a minister according to the gift of God's grace which was given me by the working of his power. To me, though I am the very least of all the saints, this grace was given, to preach to the Gentiles the unsearchable riches of Christ, and to make all men see what is the plan of the mystery hidden for ages in God who created all things; that through the church the manifold wisdom of

holy scriptures" (Rom 1:2). From the perspective of scripture, as clearly delineated in Deuteronomy, any novelty is a condemnable "heresy."

From all the preceding it stands to reason, then, to forego later theological terminology and read the Christological passage of Philippians functionally, that is, in context, as well as scripturally. If God's "chosen one" through whom he implements his purpose is as obedient as a faithful slave, then so would be all those who follow God's law and teaching that the "Servant of the Lord" brings to them: "The Lord God has given me the tongue of those who are taught, that I may know how to sustain with a word him that is weary ... Who among you fears the Lord and obeys the voice of his servant, who walks in darkness and has no light, yet trusts in the name of the Lord and relies upon his God?" (Is 50:4, 10) The company of the Servant's followers obviously includes the "evangelizer" who is to herald God's plan to the nations as well as to Jerusalem. This is precisely how Paul ended up presenting himself and the Lord Jesus Christ as examples to be followed by the Philippians. In later verses, foreseeing his own "absence," he will apply the same rule to Timothy, his heir in the leadership of all his churches, including that of Philippi (Phil 2:19-23). After Paul is gone, the Philippians will have no excuse to relax: Timothy will make sure to remind them of that in word and in deed.

God might now be made known to the principalities and powers in the heavenly places. This was according to the eternal purpose which he has realized in Christ Jesus our Lord, in whom we have boldness and confidence of access through our faith in him."

So the questions that remain are: "Whose antitype is Christ in the hymn?" "Who in scripture 'was in the form of God' and acted in a manner as to cling to his equality with God in an egotistic way?" "Is there any indication that we have a clue in the Book of Isaiah itself?" The first "icon" that comes to mind, and correctly so, is that of the king who is God's main foe, whether it is Uzziah (Is 6) or Ahaz (ch. 7) or Hezekiah (ch. 39). Actually, the book's title points out that God commissioned Isaiah to speak "against[22] Judah and Jerusalem in the days of Uzziah, Jotham, Ahaz, and Hezekiah, kings of Judah" (1:1). Suffice it here to adduce two scriptural texts that speak of the king as a "divine being," one being from Isaiah: "My heart overflows with a goodly theme; I address my verses to the king; my tongue is like the pen of a ready scribe ... Your throne, O God, endures for ever and ever" (Ps 45:1, 6); "For to us a child is born, to us a son is given; and the government will be upon his shoulder, and his name will be called 'Wonderful Counselor, Mighty God, Everlasting Father, Prince of Peace.'" (Is 9:6) Thus, unlike the kings of Judah who were disobedient servants to the one they represented, the Suffering Servant will be the new everlasting leader through whom God's law will be implemented.

However, there is another medium whereby the request of obedience applies to Christ and the Philippians *on the same level,* which would make of Christ an immediate challenge to them and an example they must follow. Here again, the source is Isaiah who has all along been in Paul's purview when writing this

---

[22] This is one of the more common connotations of the preposition *'al,* especially in the Prophetic books.

letter. Given that the heavenly Zion is to be the city of God whose light will guide the nations as well as Israel, the message of Second-Isaiah includes express references, in conjunction with the new Zion, not only to Abraham (Is 41:8; 51:2) through whom all nations shall be blessed (Gen 12:3), but also to Noah (54:9) and even Eden (51:3) and Adam (45:12). However, while the references to Abraham, Noah, and Eden are positive, the one dealing with Adam reflects his "revolt" against his "maker out of clay" in Genesis 2-3:

> Woe to him who strives with *his Maker* (*yoṣero*), an earthen vessel with the potter! Does the clay say to *him who fashions it* (*yoṣero*), "What are you making?" or "Your work has no handles?" Woe to him who says to a father, "What are you begetting?" or to a woman, "With what are you in travail?" Thus says the Lord, the Holy One of Israel, and his Maker (*yoṣero*): "Will you question me about my children, or command me concerning the work of my hands?" I made the earth, and created (*bara'ti*) man upon it; it was my hands that stretched out the heavens, and I commanded all their host. (Is 45:9-12)[23]

On the other hand, in the call describing the way of entry into God's city, the invitation is extended to every "man," including the foreigner and the eunuch, to become God's "servant (slave)":

> Thus says the Lord: "Keep justice, and do righteousness, for soon my salvation will come, and my deliverance be revealed. Blessed is *the man* who does this, and *the son of man* who holds it fast, who keeps the sabbath, not profaning it, and keeps his hand from doing any evil. Let not the foreigner who has joined himself to the

---

[23] We have here the two verbs *bara'* (create) and *yaṣar* (form out of the ground) found in Genesis 1:27 and 2:7, respectively, to describe God's action when making the human being.

Lord say, 'The Lord will surely separate me from his people'; and let not the eunuch say, 'Behold, I am a dry tree.'" For thus says the Lord: "To the eunuchs who keep my sabbaths, who choose the things that please me and hold fast my covenant, I will give in my house and within my walls a monument and a name better than sons and daughters; I will give them an everlasting name which shall not be cut off. And the foreigners who join themselves to the Lord, to minister to him, to love the name of the Lord, and to be *his servants*, every one who keeps the sabbath, and does not profane it, and holds fast my covenant— these I will bring to my holy mountain, and make them joyful in my house of prayer; their burnt offerings and their sacrifices will be accepted on my altar; for my house shall be called a house of prayer for all peoples." (Is 56:1-7)

This universal call is actually the main point of Third-Isaiah (Is 56-66) since it forms an *inclusio* bracketing this entire section (56:20-21) before ending in the announcement of the establishment of "the new heavens and the new earth" (66:22-23). The importance of this message can be seen in the Pentateuch where God's law is presented as the bread of life for *ha'dam* (the man, every man) in Deuteronomy: "... that he might make you know that man (*ha'dam*) does not live by bread alone, but that man (*ha'dam*) lives by everything that proceeds out of the mouth of the Lord." (8:3)

The seed of this scriptural view was already planted by Ezekiel, "the father of scripture."[24] That prophet's staunch anti-kingly stand is evident in that it was a "son of man" who was chosen to

---

[24] See *OTI*, 29-40.

lead the people when the "son of God," the king, was punished into exile (Ezek 1:1-3; 2:1). Furthermore, this "son of man" reminded his people, the Judahites, that after all they were similar to the human beings surrounding them: "Your origin and your birth are of the land of the Canaanites; your father was an Amorite, and your mother a Hittite." (16:2; see also v.45) The only difference was that they were "entrusted with *ta logia tou theou* (God's law inscribed in the words of the Torah)" (Rom 3:2). This thesis is taken up in the Torah itself (Pentateuch) which begins with the first 11 chapters of Genesis where Abraham's origins are anchored within total humanity. From the beginning, Adam is presented along the lines of the disobedient Israel: though he was created and formed by God, he opted to disregard the divine commandment (Gen 2:16-17), which transgression earned him punishment away from the tree of life. It is understandable then that the Isaianic Suffering Servant, whose mission included the nations as well as Israel, that is, the entire humanity, be presented as a counterpart not only to the Judahite kings, but to the disobedient "human being" as well. He is, at the same time, the new David and the new Adam, and this teaching was picked up by Paul (Rom 5; 1 Cor 15). This functional connection between David the King and Adam the Man as misguided and disobedient "leaders" is rooted in scripture. Ezekiel's approach found its way into the creation narrative where the human being is addressed in the same terminology as a monarch by its deity:

> Then God said, "Let us make man in our image, after our likeness; and let them *have dominion* over the fish of the sea, and over the birds of the air, and over the cattle, and over all the earth, and over

every creeping thing that creeps upon the earth." So God created man in his own image, in the image of God he created him; male and female he created them. And God blessed them, and God said to them, "Be fruitful and multiply, and fill the earth and *subdue* it; and *have dominion* over the fish of the sea and over the birds of the air and over every living thing that moves upon the earth." (Gen 1:26-28)[25]

The responsibility that each of the Philippians has, or must have, will be heard a few verses later: "… for God is at work in you, both to will and to work for his good pleasure. Do all things without grumbling or questioning, that you may be blameless and innocent, children of God without blemish in the midst of a crooked and perverse generation, *among whom you shine as lights in the world*." (Phil 2:13-15) In the absence of a king, each and every member of God's people has full responsibility to be his "holy one": "Say to *all the congregation of the people of Israel*, You shall be holy; for I the Lord your God am holy. *Every one of you* shall revere his mother and his father, and you shall keep my sabbaths: I am the Lord your God." (Lev 19:2-3)

All the preceding shows that the writer of the epistle followed Isaiah's lead in showing that the Suffering Servant was the "new Adam" in his complete and total obedience: he succeeded where the first Adam had miserably failed. In so doing, the writer locked more firmly the parallelism between Christ and the Philippians: both he and they are ultimately "children of Adam"

---

[25] See also Gen 2:19-20: "So out of the ground the Lord God formed every beast of the field and every bird of the air, and brought them to the man to see what he would call them; and whatever the man called every living creature, that was its name. The man gave names to all cattle, and to the birds of the air, and to every beast of the field."

bound to obedience to God. Though Adam was similar to God in that he was created in his "image (*eikōn*) and likeness (*homoiōsis*)" he had to remember that he was still human, and thus destructible, and not cling to this prerogative as though it was something he could hold onto as properly his. Actually, in Isaiah 40:18-20 the terms "image (*eikōn*)" and "likeness (*homoiōma*)" are found in reference to *assumed* deities. If the writer of Philippians preferred "form" (*morphē*) over "image" (*eikōn*), it is because it suited better his purpose: he could build on it more easily in Greek. Later, he will use the compounds *symmorphozomenos* to speak of Paul's becoming like Christ (Phil 3:10) and *symmorphon* to describe the likeness between our bodies and the glorious one of Christ (v.21).[26] The author did not have to look farther than Isaiah who used *morphē* in 44:13, a text also dealing with false deities.

To recapitulate, the Christological passage in Philippians is not a philisophico-theological compendium on the "person" of Christ. Rather it was conceived ad hoc by the writer to present the scriptural (Isaianic) Christ as an example of humility to be emulated by the Philippians. After all, scripture is prescriptive rather than descriptive. That is why the point of linkage between Christ and the Philippians is how to be truly a "human being": through obedience. Indeed, the two positive actions of Christ are done in conjunction with his being "human": "... but emptied himself, taking the *form* of a *servant*, being born in the *likeness of men*. And *as to shape* (form) being found as *man* he humbled

---

[26] The preposition *syn*— (like the Latin *cum*—) at the beginning of a word underscores oneness as well as a close link.

himself, becoming *obedient* unto death." (Phil 2:7-8) The intention of the imperial terminology, stressed mainly in the second part of the hymn, is to remind the Philippians, many of whom were Roman soldiers, that if their "lord" and "emperor" was an obedient slave, they, his servants, have no choice but to be obedient to him. It is in this sense that Christ in Philippians 2:6-11 is also, albeit secondarily, the Isaianic new David.

Vv. 12-18 ¹² Ὥστε, ἀγαπητοί μου, καθὼς πάντοτε ὑπηκούσατε, μὴ ὡς ἐν τῇ παρουσίᾳ μου μόνον ἀλλὰ νῦν πολλῷ μᾶλλον ἐν τῇ ἀπουσίᾳ μου, μετὰ φόβου καὶ τρόμου τὴν ἑαυτῶν σωτηρίαν κατεργάζεσθε· ¹³θεὸς γάρ ἐστιν ὁ ἐνεργῶν ἐν ὑμῖν καὶ τὸ θέλειν καὶ τὸ ἐνεργεῖν ὑπὲρ τῆς εὐδοκίας. ¹⁴Πάντα ποιεῖτε χωρὶς γογγυσμῶν καὶ διαλογισμῶν, ¹⁵ἵνα γένησθε ἄμεμπτοι καὶ ἀκέραιοι, τέκνα θεοῦ ἄμωμα μέσον γενεᾶς σκολιᾶς καὶ διεστραμμένης, ἐν οἷς φαίνεσθε ὡς φωστῆρες ἐν κόσμῳ, ¹⁶λόγον ζωῆς ἐπέχοντες, εἰς καύχημα ἐμοὶ εἰς ἡμέραν Χριστοῦ, ὅτι οὐκ εἰς κενὸν ἔδραμον οὐδὲ εἰς κενὸν ἐκοπίασα. ¹⁷Ἀλλὰ εἰ καὶ σπένδομαι ἐπὶ τῇ θυσίᾳ καὶ λειτουργίᾳ τῆς πίστεως ὑμῶν, χαίρω καὶ συγχαίρω πᾶσιν ὑμῖν· ¹⁸τὸ δὲ αὐτὸ καὶ ὑμεῖς χαίρετε καὶ συγχαίρετέ μοι.

¹²Therefore, my beloved, as you have always obeyed, so now, not only as in my presence but much more in my absence, work out your own salvation with fear and trembling; ¹³for God is at work in you, both to will and to work for his good pleasure. ¹⁴Do all things without grumbling or questioning, ¹⁵that you may be blameless and innocent, children of God without blemish in the midst of a crooked and perverse generation, among whom you shine as lights in the world, ¹⁶holding fast the word of life, so that in the day of Christ I may be proud that I did not run in vain or labor in vain. [17]Even if I am to be poured as a libation upon the sacrificial offering of your faith, I am glad and rejoice with you all. [18]Likewise you also should be glad and rejoice with me.

On the basis of the preceding Paul urges the Philippians to proceed on the way they started (1:5), though here he uses the notion of "obedience" he introduced in 2:6-11. They are to continue even in his absence, that is, after his own death, since the salvation they are yearning for will not be implemented until Christ is revealed as the savior at his coming (3:20). And since that coming will usher God's judgment (1:10; 2:15), they will have to work out fully (*katergazesthe*) the prerequisites that will allow them to be part of the savior's party. However, they should not be fooled into imagining that "working out fully their salvation" is their own doing. It is rather "he [God] who *began* a good work (*ergon*) in you" who "will *bring it to completion* at the day of Jesus Christ" (1:6). Paul makes sure that the Philippians understand that their "work" lies rather in *obedience* to the one who alone is the "worker" (*energōn*) of his "good pleasure" (*eudokias*) in that he implements his pleasure in triggering the Philippians to will (*thelein*) and in sustaining them to work (*energein*) toward that aim. Even Paul himself will be bound to this rule (3:12-14). The Philippians are no—ought not to be— better than the Suffering Servant in whom God's "good pleasure" prospers because it was God's "good pleasure" to bruise him: "Yet it was the *good pleasure (delight, will)* of the Lord to bruise him; he has put him to grief; when he makes himself an offering for sin, he shall see his offspring, he shall prolong his days; the *good pleasure (delight, will)* of the Lord shall prosper in his hand." (Is 53:10) Paul is consistent in that, earlier when referring to those who shared, with good intention, in his apostolic mission, which started according to God's *evdokia* (good pleasure),[27] they were said to be acting *di' evdokian*, in view of (or due to) the (divine) good pleasure (Phil 1:15).

Since the Philippians, being slaves, have no say but to do their Lord's will, they ought to do so "without grumbling or questioning" (2:14), especially in view of the coming reckoning when they will have to be found "blameless and innocent, without blemish" (vv.15-16; see also earlier 1:10). Their behavior is to be that of Roman slaves, who are "children" of their master in the sense that they are part of his household[28] and thus represent him to the outside world; their behavior reflects on him. The witness of such behavior will be toward the Jews who oppose Paul's teaching as well as toward the Gentiles. The term "world" (*kosmos*) in the New Testament refers usually to the universe, and more specifically to the (world of the) Roman empire at large, in the same way as "earth" (*gē*) indicates the entire inhabited universe, and more specifically the Roman "habitation" (*oikoumenē [gē]*). As for Paul's opponents and their followers, they are intended in the phrase "(children of God without blemish) in the midst of a crooked and perverse generation," which harks back word for word to the statement in Deuteronomy where the children of Israel are criticized thus: "They have dealt corruptly with him, they are no longer his children because of their blemish; they are a crooked and perverse generation." (32:5)[29] This phraseology already prepares

---

[27] See also Gal 1:15-16 (But when he who had set me apart before I was born, and had called me through his grace, *was pleased* [*evdokēsen*] to reveal his Son to me, in order that I might preach him among the Gentiles, I did not confer with flesh and blood).

[28] This explains the ease with which Paul moves between referring to his addressees as slaves of God and his children (Rom 6-8).

[29] This, in a nutshell, is the thesis defended in Rom 9-11.

for what Paul will say a few verses later to the effect that his followers are said to be "the true circumcision, who worship God in spirit, and glory in Christ Jesus, and put no confidence in the flesh" (Phil 3:3), immediately after the caveat "Look out for the dogs, look out for the evil-workers, look out for those who mutilate the flesh" (v.2). The same thought occurs at the end of the passage where Paul presents himself as the example of the "truthful Jew" (Rom 2:28-29) for the Philippians to follow:

> Brethren, join in imitating me, and mark those who so live as you have an example in us. For many, of whom I have often told you and now tell you even with tears, live as enemies of the cross of Christ. Their end is destruction, their god is the belly, and they glory in their shame, with minds set on earthly things. (Phil 3:17-19)

The Philippians are asked "to shine as lights (*phainesthe hōs phōstēres*) in the world" (2:15). This is an undisputable reference to Daniel's "those who are wise shall *shine like the lights* (*phanousin hōs phōstēres*) of the heaven" (12:3) since these are the sole instances of *phōstēres* (lights) referring to human beings rather than the heavenly bodies (sun, moon, and stars) in the Bible. The Daniel link is also confirmed in that, in both instances, the reference to being "lights" is made in conjunction with the last judgment where those who are supposed to be "lights" will be shown to be indeed so only after the test. Consequently, the Philippians are not asked here to be proponents of the gospel teaching as its teachers, but rather as its doers; the only indicative tense verb of the principal clause is the imperative "do" (*poieite*; Phil 2:14). The only other indicative tense verbs in the sentence (vv.14-16) are found in the subordinate clause referring to Paul's toiling for the sake of the gospel: "that I did not run in vain or labor in vain." (v.16)[30] Consequently, "holding fast to the word of life" is not a mental exercise through which one expresses the right creedal formula. As was alluded to earlier in Deuteronomy, it is living according to God's "word of the law" that was prescribed unto life for whoever will have been obedient to its commandments, but can also prove to be unto death for whoever does not abide by them. Indeed, if the Philippians behave as Paul ordered, the result will be not their boast, but his boast in the sense that he will appear "on the day of Christ" as God's true apostle (v.16).

However, even if he is poured as a libation over his sacrificial liturgical offering, which is the Philippians' trust in the gospel he preached to them, Paul will rejoice in that together with them. This is the classical Pauline linkage between suffering for the sake of the gospel and sharing in the eschatological joy it provides, since its message entails the ushering in as well the announcement of the Jerusalem above, God's new city.[31] He is thus inviting the Philippians to rejoice and share in his joy. In so doing he is summoning them to take their gaze away from his being in prison and their eventual orphanhood in case he dies, and to concentrate rather on the joy of the Kingdom which they will eventually share together. Such an attitude will be proof of their trust in his preaching and, by the same token, that he was successful in it. That is to say, if they rejoice with him now, this

---

[30] As is clear from Gal 2:2 (I laid before them [but privately before those who were of repute] the gospel which I preach among the Gentiles, lest somehow I should be running or had run in vain).

[31] Gal 4:26-5:1.

will guarantee that they will rejoice with him later (1:18). Our actual expression of joy in view of the Kingdom is a sign, not that we are already there, but simply that we have put our trust in God's promise, which is the basis of the real test on which we shall be graciously granted inheritance in the Kingdom when it comes:

> Therefore, since we are justified by faith (trust in God's gospel word of promise), we have peace with God through our Lord Jesus Christ. Through him *we have obtained access to this grace* in which we stand, and *we rejoice in our hope of sharing the glory of God.* More than that, *we rejoice in our sufferings*, knowing that *suffering produces* endurance, and endurance produces character, and character produces *hope, and hope does not disappoint us*, because God's love has been poured into our hearts through the Holy Spirit which has been given to us. (Rom 5:1-5)

This reading is corroborated by the fact that the only other instance of *spendomai* (I am poured out as a libation) occurs in 2 Timothy 4:5-7 in conjunction with Paul's impending death: "As for you, always be steady, endure suffering, do the work of an evangelist, fulfill your ministry. For I am already *on the point of being sacrificed* (*spendomai*); the time of my departure has come. I have fought the good fight, I have finished the race, I have kept the faith (trust)."

On another note, this temple terminology occurs in Romans in full parallelism with that of Paul's apostolic activity:

> But on some points I have written to you very boldly by way of reminder, because of the grace given me by God to be a *liturg* (*leitourgon*) of Christ Jesus to the Gentiles, *hierourgizing* (*hierourgounta*) the gospel of God, so that the *offering* (*prosphora*)

of the Gentiles may be acceptable, sanctified by the Holy Spirit. In Christ Jesus, then, I have reason to be proud of my work for God. For I will not venture to speak of anything except what Christ has wrought through me to win obedience from the Gentiles, by word and deed, by the power of signs and wonders, by the power of the Holy Spirit, so that from Jerusalem and as far round as Illyricum I have fully preached the gospel of Christ, thus making it my ambition to preach the gospel, not where Christ has already been named, lest I build on another man's foundation, but as it is written, "They shall see who have never been told of him, and they shall understand who have never heard of him." (15:15-21)

I have quoted the entire passage in order to show that the context is clearly one of apostolic activity. It is then *as apostle* that Paul views himself as the liturgizing high priest of what he referred to earlier in the epistle as sacrifice (*thysian*) and *word-y* worship (*logikēn latreian*; Rom 12:2), that is, a worship rendered through and in conjunction with the "gospel word." The conclusion is unavoidable. Paul is the high priest of the heavenly temple whose liturgy is celebrated in every house-church under the aegis of the Lord Jesus as preached according to the one gospel whose sole faithful apostle is Paul and after Paul, Timothy, as we shall hear in the following verses.

Vv. 19-24 ¹⁹ Ἐλπίζω δὲ ἐν κυρίῳ Ἰησοῦ Τιμόθεον ταχέως πέμψαι ὑμῖν, ἵνα κἀγὼ εὐψυχῶ γνοὺς τὰ περὶ ὑμῶν. ²⁰οὐδένα γὰρ ἔχω ἰσόψυχον, ὅστις γνησίως τὰ περὶ ὑμῶν μεριμνήσει· ²¹οἱ πάντες γὰρ τὰ ἑαυτῶν ζητοῦσιν, οὐ τὰ Ἰησοῦ Χριστοῦ. ²²τὴν δὲ δοκιμὴν αὐτοῦ γινώσκετε, ὅτι ὡς πατρὶ τέκνον σὺν ἐμοὶ ἐδούλευσεν εἰς τὸ εὐαγγέλιον. ²³τοῦτον μὲν οὖν ἐλπίζω πέμψαι ὡς ἂν ἀφίδω τὰ περὶ ἐμὲ ἐξαυτῆς· ²⁴πέποιθα δὲ ἐν κυρίῳ ὅτι καὶ αὐτὸς ταχέως ἐλεύσομαι.

¹⁹I hope in the Lord Jesus to send Timothy to you soon, so that I may be cheered by news of you. ²⁰I have no one like him, who will be genuinely anxious for your welfare. ²¹They all look after their own interests, not those of Jesus Christ. ²² But Timothy's worth you know, how as a son with a father he has served with me in the gospel. ²³I hope therefore to send him just as soon as I see how it will go with me; ²⁴and I trust in the Lord that shortly I myself shall come also.

If Paul has "made it" since he is about to be "absent" from them—either by dying or by lingering a while more in jail—the Philippians are still "on the way." That is why Paul is sending them Timothy, his heir, from the heavenly city where he performs his service, in order to learn of their perseverance toward the goal of joining him in the joy of the Kingdom. Timothy is presented as the unequalled trustworthy person: he is *isopsykhon* (equal in soul, soulmate; Phil 2:20) with Paul given that he has genuinely at heart the matters concerning the Philippians to the extent that, should his report be positive, then Paul's "soul" would be fully relieved (*evpsykhō*).³² The connotation is clear: Timothy is another Paul. Furthermore, he is someone who is not self-serving (v.21) and will look after the matters of Jesus Christ. This statement recalls what Paul wrote earlier:

> Some indeed preach Christ from envy and rivalry, but others from good will. The latter do it out of love, knowing that I am put here for the defense of the gospel; the former proclaim Christ out of

---

³² Notice the intended wordplay between *evpsykhō* and *isopsykhon*, both built on the root *psykhē* (soul). The link is made even tighter through the repetition of *ta peri hymōn* (the matters concerning you) with each of *evpsykhō* and *isopsykhon*.

partisanship, not sincerely but thinking to afflict me in my imprisonment. (1:15-17)

Finally, in order to underscore that his evaluation of Timothy is not subjective, Paul appeals to the fact that the Philippians themselves know that Timothy passed the "test" (*dokimēn*; 2:22a) to the extent that he acted as a "slave" to the gospel together with Paul himself (v.22b; see also 1:1), showing thus that he is a genuine child to the Apostle.[33] As that kind of child, he is the right choice to instruct and lead God's children, the Philippians, into behaving according to their heavenly Father's will (1:15) in a genuine manner.

As he has done time and again in this epistle, Paul ends on a note that prepares the Philippians for the eventuality of their not seeing him. Just before expressing his trust that he too would be coming their way *soon* (2:24; compare with 1:25-26), he hints to the fact that sending Timothy *soon* (2:19) and *exavtēs* (at once; immediately; as soon as; v.23) may be delayed until after Paul has seen how it will go with him, that is, the decision concerning either his release or his death. This is clearly a literary device to say that most probably the Philippians will not see Paul or even Timothy again. Indeed, if Paul is to be released, then there is no need for him to send Timothy since he himself would be coming to them. If the decision is his execution, then Timothy will need to remain in Ephesus to take Paul's place at the helm at the Pauline headquarters (1 Tim 1:3). This is precisely why he is "sending" his testament to them in writing. Actually, Paul's

---

[33] The combination of *gnēsiōs* (genuinely) and *teknon* (child) found in Phil 2:21-22 concerning Timothy occurs also in 1 Tim 1:2.

assuredness (*pepoitha*; Phil 2:24) that the Philippians will be taken care of is beyond himself and Timothy and is in God's hands: "And I am sure (*pepoithōs*) that he who *began* a good work in you will bring it to *completion* at the day of Jesus Christ." (1:6).

Vv. ***25-30*** ²⁵ Ἀναγκαῖον δὲ ἡγησάμην Ἐπαφρόδιτον τὸν ἀδελφὸν καὶ συνεργὸν καὶ συστρατιώτην μου, ὑμῶν δὲ ἀπόστολον καὶ λειτουργὸν τῆς χρείας μου, πέμψαι πρὸς ὑμᾶς, ²⁶ἐπειδὴ ἐπιποθῶν ἦν πάντας ὑμᾶς καὶ ἀδημονῶν, διότι ἠκούσατε ὅτι ἠσθένησεν. ²⁷καὶ γὰρ ἠσθένησεν παραπλήσιον θανάτῳ· ἀλλὰ ὁ θεὸς ἠλέησεν αὐτόν, οὐκ αὐτὸν δὲ μόνον ἀλλὰ καὶ ἐμέ, ἵνα μὴ λύπην ἐπὶ λύπην σχῶ. ²⁸σπουδαιοτέρως οὖν ἔπεμψα αὐτόν, ἵνα ἰδόντες αὐτὸν πάλιν χαρῆτε κἀγὼ ἀλυπότερος ὦ. ²⁹προσδέχεσθε οὖν αὐτὸν ἐν κυρίῳ μετὰ πάσης χαρᾶς καὶ τοὺς τοιούτους ἐντίμους ἔχετε, ³⁰ὅτι διὰ τὸ ἔργον Χριστοῦ μέχρι θανάτου ἤγγισεν παραβολευσάμενος τῇ ψυχῇ, ἵνα ἀναπληρώσῃ τὸ ὑμῶν ὑστέρημα τῆς πρός με λειτουργίας.

²⁵*I have thought it necessary to send to you Epaphroditus my brother and fellow worker and fellow soldier, and your messenger and minister to my need,* ²⁶*for he has been longing for you all, and has been distressed because you heard that he was ill.* ²⁷*Indeed he was ill, near to death. But God had mercy on him, and not only on him but on me also, lest I should have sorrow upon sorrow.* ²⁸*I am the more eager to send him, therefore, that you may rejoice at seeing him again, and that I may be less anxious.* ²⁹*So receive him in the Lord with all joy; and honor such men,* ³⁰*for he nearly died for the work of Christ, risking his life to complete your service to me.*

This reading is corroborated in that, immediately, Paul invites the Philippians to shift their attention away from Timothy to his plan of "sending" Epaphroditus to them by referring to it as "necessary" (*anankaion*; 2:25). This notion of necessity is linked to apostolic activity as one can see from its use in 1 Corinthians 9:16-17: "For if I preach the gospel, that gives me no ground for boasting. For necessity (*anankē*) is laid upon me. Woe to me if I do not preach the gospel! For if I do this of my own will, I have a reward; but if not of my own will, I am entrusted with a commission (*oikonomian*)."[34] But, already earlier in Philippians, we encountered the adjective *anankaioteron* (more necessary) in conjunction with Paul's referring to his apostolic duty toward the Philippians: "But to remain in the flesh is more necessary on your account." (Phil 1:24) On the other hand, one is struck by the change in the use of both the verbs and their tenses. Whereas Paul "hopes (is hoping)" *twice* to send Timothy (2:19, 23), he already "considered"[35] it necessary to send Epaphroditus. Furthermore, the verb "considered" (*hēgēsamēn*) is the same as the one used in this letter in conjunction with the behavior required by the "gospel teaching" of Isaiah, whether it applies to the Philippians (v.3), Christ (v.6) or Paul (3:7, 8 [twice]). Thus, when "hearing" the epistle read to them, the Philippians will have to be convinced that Paul's decision to send them Epaphroditus instead of Timothy, and even instead of his coming to them himself, was not made conveniently, let alone haphazardly, but *according to the gospel* in which they have

---

[34] *oikonomia* is the duty of the *oikonomos*, the slave in charge of his master's household and who reports directly to him.

[35] The aorist (*hēgēsamēn*) reflects a final decision.

partnership from the beginning (1:5). They will have to submit to Paul's decision "without grumbling or questioning" (2:14). What a tour de force on the writer's end!

That Paul is sending Epaphroditus *instead of* Timothy can be seen in the heaping of five titles in a row to speak of Epaphroditus, a unique case in the New Testament. The first three are specifically Timothean, so to speak. When together, the first two, brother and co-worker, are reserved to Timothy elsewhere and in a similar context: "Therefore when we could bear it no longer, we were willing to be left behind at Athens alone, and we sent Timothy, our brother and God's servant in the gospel of Christ, to establish you in your faith and to exhort you, that no one be moved by these afflictions." (1 Thess 3:1-3) The parallelism is unmistakable and actually striking when one recalls that Thessalonica and Philippi are both Macedonian cities. On the other hand, Epaphroditus is Paul's only helper who is introduced by the Apostle himself as his co-soldier (*systratiōtēn*),[36] besides Timothy: "Share in harsh suffering (*synkakopathēson*) as a good soldier of Christ Jesus." (2 Tim 2:2)[37] Epaphroditus is then Paul's emissary to the Philippians in the same way and with the same value as Timothy is to the Thessalonians. Since Epaphroditus would be going to Philippi in place of Timothy, he had to be "exalted" in the eyes of his community to appear on a par with Timothy and even Paul,

---

[36] This choice of noun may have been dictated by the fact that most of the Philippians were Roman soldiers.

[37] The parallelism is evident in the Greek through the preposition *syn*— in either case, once at the beginning of the noun co-soldier and the other time at the beginning of the verb "suffer badly."

especially since he was a Philippian and "a prophet is not without honor, except in his own country, and among his own kin, and in his own house" (Mk 6:4). The parity with Timothy seems to be subtly iterated at the end of the passage where Paul writes that the likes of Epaphroditus are to be held by the Philippians *entimous* (in honor; Phil 2:29), which is from the same root *tim*— as *Timotheos* (Timothy).

Still, sending Epaphroditus amounted actually to returning him to the Philippians who had sent him Paul's way in the first place. That would mean that Paul was refusing their "gift" (*doma*) to him (4:17). However, as he will also assert, he made an exception in this matter to the Philippians since he does not usually accept any gift from his churches (v.15; see also 1 Cor 9:1-15). So he turns the tables by letting them know that their gift reached him fully: "for he [Epaphroditus] nearly died for the work of Christ, risking his life to complete (fulfill) the lack (need; *to hysterēma*) of your liturgy to me." (Phil 2:30) By calling their gift to him a "liturgy," however, he was actually letting them know that their actual gift to him lay in their having accepted him as their apostle, that is, their high priest in the heavenly Zion. And it is he who is "sending" them back from his "chains" their "apostle" Epaphroditus transformed into another co-worker of his, the equal of the unequalled Timothy, in order to lead them further, as an "apostle" of God would, on the path of the gospel toward God's city. Indeed, their original "liturgy toward me [Paul]" had "its lack (need)" (*to hysterēma*); however, as Paul will write later, the Philippians' true "gift" is "*the fruit* (of

Paul's "gospel labor") that did increase to their credit" (4:17).[38]
He goes about this matter later in a magisterially written passage.

Just as Epaphroditus ⟶

This transformation of Epaphroditus was ultimately God's
work as Paul wrote earlier in 2:12-13. As an offering by the
Philippians for the cause of Paul's gospel, Epahroditus
underwent the test of becoming "a fragrant offering, a sacrifice
acceptable and pleasing to God" (4:18) by suffering, while in
Paul's service, an illness that almost brought about his death "for
the work of Christ" (2:30). Such an experience made him equal
to Paul, who is about "to be poured as a libation upon the
sacrificial offering of the Philippians' trust in God" (2:17). Had
Epaphroditus died, it would have been to the sorrow of Paul
since he would have had no one to lead the Philippians on the
remainder of their trek toward the Kingdom. But God was
merciful and preserved Epaphroditus to allow Paul to fulfill his
hope and rejoice together with the Philippians: "But God had
mercy on him, and not only on him but on me also, lest I should
have sorrow upon sorrow. I am the more eager to send him,
therefore, that you may rejoice at seeing him again, and that I
may be less sorrowful." (vv.27-28) Thus Paul vindicated his
sending Epaphroditus back to them without hurting their
feelings. Such sending was an expression of the "fruit" of God's
gospel preached by Paul, which is a "logic-al worship": what we
imagine we are offering to God is merely his having offered us
his word of instruction unto salvation. Paradoxically, our
offering can only be "thanksgiving" (*evkharistia*), as Paul will
write later: "Have no anxiety about anything, but in everything

---

[38] See further my comments on Phil 4:15-20 below.

by prayer and supplication *with thanksgiving* let your requests be made known to God." (4:6)

Given all of this concerning Epaphroditus, one cannot but wonder if his name is not intentionally symbolic, as are the majority, if not all, of the names in the New Testament. The Greek *epaphroditos*[39] is an adjective meaning "filled with pleasure (blessing, fortune)," and thus "bestowing pleasure (blessing, fortune)," its counterpart in Latin being *felix* (felicitous, fortunate, blessed). Thus Epaphroditus is the consummate "fortunate" someone who is blessed by God in order to bestow those blessings, in turn, on the Philippians.

① Just as Epaphroditus (one of his was transformed from a Roman citizen into a citizen of the heavenly kingdom, the Philippians can also be transformed

---

[39] The Greek root is the name Aphrodite, the goddess of love and felicity.

Chapter 3

Vv. 1-16 ¹Τὸ λοιπόν, ἀδελφοί μου, χαίρετε ἐν κυρίῳ. τὰ αὐτὰ γράφειν ὑμῖν ἐμοὶ μὲν οὐκ ὀκνηρόν, ὑμῖν δὲ ἀσφαλές. ²Βλέπετε τοὺς κύνας, βλέπετε τοὺς κακοὺς ἐργάτας, βλέπετε τὴν κατατομήν. ³ἡμεῖς γάρ ἐσμεν ἡ περιτομή, οἱ πνεύματι θεοῦ λατρεύοντες καὶ καυχώμενοι ἐν Χριστῷ Ἰησοῦ καὶ οὐκ ἐν σαρκὶ πεποιθότες, ⁴καίπερ ἐγὼ ἔχων πεποίθησιν καὶ ἐν σαρκί. Εἴ τις δοκεῖ ἄλλος πεποιθέναι ἐν σαρκί, ἐγὼ μᾶλλον· ⁵περιτομῇ ὀκταήμερος, ἐκ γένους Ἰσραήλ, φυλῆς Βενιαμίν, Ἑβραῖος ἐξ Ἑβραίων, κατὰ νόμον Φαρισαῖος, ⁶κατὰ ζῆλος διώκων τὴν ἐκκλησίαν, κατὰ δικαιοσύνην τὴν ἐν νόμῳ γενόμενος ἄμεμπτος. ⁷[Ἀλλὰ] ἄτινα ἦν μοι κέρδη, ταῦτα ἥγημαι διὰ τὸν Χριστὸν ζημίαν. ⁸ἀλλὰ μενοῦνγε καὶ ἡγοῦμαι πάντα ζημίαν εἶναι διὰ τὸ ὑπερέχον τῆς γνώσεως Χριστοῦ Ἰησοῦ τοῦ κυρίου μου, δι' ὃν τὰ πάντα ἐζημιώθην, καὶ ἡγοῦμαι σκύβαλα, ἵνα Χριστὸν κερδήσω ⁹καὶ εὑρεθῶ ἐν αὐτῷ, μὴ ἔχων ἐμὴν δικαιοσύνην τὴν ἐκ νόμου ἀλλὰ τὴν διὰ πίστεως Χριστοῦ, τὴν ἐκ θεοῦ δικαιοσύνην ἐπὶ τῇ πίστει, ¹⁰τοῦ γνῶναι αὐτὸν καὶ τὴν δύναμιν τῆς ἀναστάσεως αὐτοῦ καὶ [τὴν] κοινωνίαν [τῶν] παθημάτων αὐτοῦ, συμμορφιζόμενος τῷ θανάτῳ αὐτοῦ, ¹¹εἴ πως καταντήσω εἰς τὴν ἐξανάστασιν τὴν ἐκ νεκρῶν. ¹²Οὐχ ὅτι ἤδη ἔλαβον ἢ ἤδη τετελείωμαι, διώκω δὲ εἰ καὶ καταλάβω, ἐφ' ᾧ καὶ κατελήμφθην ὑπὸ Χριστοῦ [Ἰησοῦ]. ¹³ἀδελφοί, ἐγὼ ἐμαυτὸν οὐ λογίζομαι κατειληφέναι· ἓν δέ, τὰ μὲν ὀπίσω ἐπιλανθανόμενος τοῖς δὲ ἔμπροσθεν ἐπεκτεινόμενος, ¹⁴κατὰ σκοπὸν διώκω εἰς τὸ βραβεῖον τῆς ἄνω κλήσεως τοῦ θεοῦ ἐν Χριστῷ Ἰησοῦ. ¹⁵Ὅσοι οὖν τέλειοι, τοῦτο φρονῶμεν· καὶ εἴ τι ἑτέρως φρονεῖτε, καὶ τοῦτο ὁ θεὸς ὑμῖν ἀποκαλύψει· ¹⁶πλὴν εἰς ὃ ἐφθάσαμεν, τῷ αὐτῷ στοιχεῖν.

¹Finally, my brethren, rejoice in the Lord. To write the same things to you is not irksome to me, and is safe for you. ²Look out for the dogs, look out for the evil-workers, look out for those who

149

mutilate the flesh. ³For we are the true circumcision, who worship God in spirit, and glory in Christ Jesus, and put no confidence in the flesh. ⁴Though I myself have reason for confidence in the flesh also. If any other man thinks he has reason for confidence in the flesh, I have more: ⁵circumcised on the eighth day, of the people of Israel, of the tribe of Benjamin, a Hebrew born of Hebrews; as to the law a Pharisee, ⁶as to zeal a persecutor of the church, as to righteousness under the law blameless. ⁷ But whatever gain I had, I counted as loss for the sake of Christ. ⁸Indeed I count everything as loss because of the surpassing worth of knowing Christ Jesus my Lord. For his sake I have suffered the loss of all things, and count them as refuse, in order that I may gain Christ ⁹and be found in him, not having a righteousness of my own, based on law, but that which is through faith in Christ, the righteousness from God that depends on faith; ¹⁰that I may know him and the power of his resurrection, and may share his sufferings, becoming like him in his death, ¹¹that if possible I may attain the resurrection from the dead. ¹²Not that I have already obtained this or am already perfect; but I press on to make it my own, because Christ Jesus has made me his own. ¹³Brethren, I do not consider that I have made it my own; but one thing I do, forgetting what lies behind and straining forward to what lies ahead, ¹⁴I press on toward the goal for the prize of the upward call of God in Christ Jesus. ¹⁵Let those of us who are mature be thus minded; and if in anything you are otherwise minded, God will reveal that also to you. ¹⁶Only let us hold true to what we have attained.

The focal point Philippians is woven around is joy: in four small chapters we hear the noun "joy" and the verb "rejoice" or "rejoice with" 16 times. It appears at the beginning of the letter (1:4) and introduces (4:10) the last passage of the letter dealing with the Philippians' "gift" to Paul. It seems as though Paul is fighting throughout the letter to convince the Philippians not to worry about him and seems to have succeeded—at least on hope—when he states: "I rejoice in the Lord greatly that now at length you have revived your concern for me; you were indeed concerned for me, *but you had no opportunity.*" (4:10) The reason is simple: Paul is in jail and is trying not to allow this situation to become a source of sorrow (2:27-28). This would be unworthy of citizens of the heavenly Zion where their Lord is already reigning and preparing the banquet of rejoicing for his followers.[1]

After having presented himself and the Lord Jesus Christ as examples for the Philippians to follow, and having presented Timothy and, more especially, Epaphroditus as teachers whose teaching they are to heed, Paul moves to the content of the teaching itself, which he leaves to the Philippians as a testament and a legacy. In doing so, he follows the path he took earlier in Galatians, where the Pauline gospel is issued scripturally.[2] Just as in that letter he lay down once and for all in writing what he had earlier preached orally, here also he is committing to writing "the same things." The parallelism with Galatians is striking:

1. Paul points out his Jewishness (Phil 3:5-6; Gal 1:13-14).

2. He mentions his persecution of God's church (Phil 3:6; Gal 1:13).

3. He describes his commitment to the cause of the gospel (Phil 3:7-8; Gal 1:16-17).

---

[1] On the element "joy" in God's city see *OTI*₃ 30-32.
[2] See *NTI*₁ 35-36.

4. He reasons that the righteousness granted by God cannot be secured through the Law (Phil 3:9; Gal 2:15-21).

5. He stresses the importance of *stoikhein*, walking under (the) orders (of the Spirit) (Phil 3:16; Gal 5:25).

6. He ends up by pointing out the allegiance is to the heavenly Jerusalem whose children or citizens the believers are called to be (Phil 3:20; Gal 4:26-28).

7. He ends by asking them to "stand firm" (*stēkete*) (Phil 4:1; Gal 5:1).

However, this does not mean that Philippians 3 is a carbon copy of Galatians. Rather, as is usual in literature, it is worded in conjunction with what Paul wrote in the first two chapters. The correspondence is clear: both passages are written with joy as an *inclusio*. The first (2:3-2:30) starts with "with joy" (*meta kharas*; 2:4) and ends with "with all joy" (*meta pasēs kharas*; 2:29); the second (3:1-4:7) is bracketed with "rejoice in the Lord" (3:1) and "Rejoice in the Lord always; again I will say, Rejoice" (4:4).

 "Consigning into writing the same things" is not "irksome (bothersome)" to him since it is his duty, as an apostle, to leave in his followers' hands the "safe (secure)" (*asphales*) path to the ultimate "joy" experienced only in God's heavenly city whose citizens the Philippians are called to be (3:20). The root *asphal*— denoting assuredness (safe correctness) is a trademark which the author of Luke-Acts uses profusely to speak of the truth of the gospel he is consigning in writing. This is clear from the introduction to his two-volume work which he refers to as "words":[3]

> Inasmuch as many have undertaken to compile a narrative of the things which have been accomplished among us, just as they were delivered to us by those who from the beginning were eyewitnesses and ministers of *the word*, it seemed good to me also, having followed all things closely for some time past, to write an orderly account for you, most excellent Theophilus, that you may know the truth (*asphaleian*; assuredness, full correctness) concerning the words (*logōn*) in which you have been cathechized. (Lk 1:1-4)[4]

The introductory terminology of Philippians 3:1-4:7 thus corroborates that this passage is a rendering of the Pauline gospel whose main literary proponent is Luke.

Just as Paul asserted that those who would follow his "rule" (*kanoni*) are "the Israel of God" (Gal 6:16), here also he emphatically asserts that they are "the circumcision," that is, the true children of Abraham (Gal 3:7-9; also Rom 9:11-18). The opponents—the "dogs"—are the outsiders to the congregation of God's Israel. Following the lead of Galatians, the opponents are, in an ironic twist, accused of "mutilation of the flesh." In Galatians, the verb used is *apokopsontai* (may they cut themselves fully off; 5:12) as opposed to "be circumcised" (from *peritemnō* [cut around]).[5] Here, in Philippians, the pun is more direct since we have *katatomē* (cutting fully) as counterpart to *peritomē* (cutting around; circumcision). However, what is more important is the actual message. In Galatians, the pun concerning the "flesh" (which is circumcised) is followed by a

---

[3] Acts 1:1 (In the first book [*logon*; word], O Theophilus, I have dealt with all that Jesus began to do and teach).

[4] See my comments in *NTI₂* 25-26.

[5] Both Greek verbs *koptō* and *temnō* mean "cut."

reference to God's spirit as the new leader and whose will is to be implemented (Gal 5:16-18; 22-25). Here at center stage, between "dogs" and "cutting fully," is the phrase "evil-workers" corresponding to the "works" of the flesh in Galatians (5:19-21).

 The Philippians, on the other hand, "are the true circumcision, who worship God *in spirit*,[6] and boast in Christ Jesus, and put no confidence *in the flesh*." This shows once more that worship is not a mental formulation of the correct "creed." It is a behavior according to God's will expressed in his commandments.[7] However, the impetus behind the Philippians' correct behavior comes from God. Right at the outset of the letter Paul asserted: "And I am confident that *he who began a good work in you will bring it to completion* at the day of Jesus Christ." (Phil 1:6) And later he iterates: "Therefore, my beloved, as you have always obeyed, so now, not only as in my presence but much more in my absence, *work out* your own salvation with fear and trembling; *for God is at work* among you, *both to will and to work* for his good pleasure." (2:12-13) Thus, confidence is not in the flesh, that is, in one's self, but rather in God's spirit who leads the Philippians so long as they are *obedient* to his will. The notion of confidence[8] is used three times in a row at this juncture (3:3-4), with Galatians looming high in the background. In Galatians, at the beginning of the passage ending with the mention of "mutilation of the flesh" (Gal 5:12), there is a concentration of confidence terminology in conjunction with God's calling the Galatians through his word and asking them to proceed on the way on which they were already moving:

---

[6] Or "who worship in God's spirit," according to some manuscripts.

[7] See 1 Cor 7:19 (For neither circumcision counts for anything nor uncircumcision, but keeping the commandments of God).

[8] The verb *peithō/omai* occurs six times (1:6, 14, 25; 2:24; 3:3, 4) and the noun *pepoithēsis* once (3:4).

You were running well; who hindered you from trusting (having confidence in; *peithesthai*) the truth? This persuasion (confidence; *peismonē*[9]) is not from him who calls you. A little leaven leavens the whole lump. I have confidence (*pepoitha*) in the Lord that you will take no other view than mine; and he who is troubling you will bear his judgment, whoever he is. (Gal 5:7-10)

So also in Philippians, Paul reminds his addressees that, although he had all the reasons to be confident in his own righteousness vis-à-vis the Law (circumcised on the eighth day, of the people of Israel, of the tribe of Benjamin, a Hebrew born of Hebrews; as to the law a Pharisee, as to zeal a persecutor of the church, *as to righteousness under the law blameless*[10]; Phil 3:5-6), yet "whatever gain I had, I counted as loss for the sake of Christ" (v.7). Unfortunately, under the influence of later theology, this last statement together with the following verses (vv.8-11) have been misinterpreted along the same lines of many misinterpreted Pauline texts, especially those in Romans and Galatians, concerning the relationship between Law and grace. These misinterpretations read those texts as expressing a "full break" between the aegis of the Law and that of grace, thus creating an either-or situation. A close reading of this entire unitary section of Philippians (3:1-4:1) will help us get out of this unnecessary false impasse.

The section is clearly constructed as an *inclusio*. Paul introduces his "gospel" (3:1) and ends by inviting the Philippians to adhere to it (4:1). After advising his hearers to watch out for the opponents (3:2), he gives the reason in the first person plural "we" (v.3), that is, by including himself, the statement applies to

---

[9] This noun is from the same root as the verb *peithō/omai* and the noun *pepoithēsis*, and has the same meaning as the latter.

[10] He says as much also in 1 Cor 4:4 (I am not aware of anything against myself).

both Jews and Gentiles. Then he gives himself as an example (vv.4-11) to be followed by the Philippians (vv.17-19) before ending with the inclusive "we" again (vv.20-21). However, at the end of the passage referring to his own situation and before moving to the conclusion in which he invites the Philippians to follow his example, Paul writes the following passage where he makes the transition between the "I" and the "we":

> Not that I have already obtained this or am already perfect; but I press on to make it my own, because Christ Jesus has made me his own. Brethren, I do not consider that I have made it my own; but one thing I do, forgetting what lies behind and straining forward to what lies ahead, I press on toward the goal (*skopon*) for the prize of the upward call of God in Christ Jesus. Let those of us who are mature be thus minded; and if in anything you are otherwise minded, God will reveal that also to you on the condition that we hold true to what we have attained. Brethren, join in imitating me, and mark (*skopeite*) those who so live as you have an example in us. (3:12-17)

The imagery is that of a race in a Roman stadium where the winner is the one who crosses the finish line first and not anyone who may be ahead during the race; Aesop immortalized this teaching in his fable of the tortoise and the hare. Paul's predilection for such imagery can be seen in its ubiquitous use in his letters. As early as Galatians he applies it, as he does here, both to himself and to his addressees: "I went up by revelation; and I laid before them—but privately before those who were of repute—the gospel which I preach among the Gentiles, lest somehow I should be running or had run in vain" (2:2); "You were running well; who hindered you from obeying (trusting in; be persuaded by) the truth?" (5:7) The same occurs in 1 Corinthians and in a context similar to that in Philippians, while speaking of his apostolic mission:

I do it all for the sake of the gospel, that I may share in its blessings. Do you not know that in a race all the runners compete, but only one receives the prize? So run that you may obtain it. Every athlete (*agōnizomenos*) exercises self-control in all things. They do it to receive a perishable wreath, but we an imperishable. Well, I do not run aimlessly, I do not box as one beating the air; but I pommel my body and subdue it, lest after preaching to others I myself should be disqualified. (1 Cor 9:23-27)

In Philippians, Paul uses the same terminology in reference to both himself and his addressees:

For it has been granted to you that for the sake of Christ you should not only believe in him but also suffer for his sake, engaged in the same race (*agōn*) which you saw and now hear to be mine ... Let each of you look (*skopountes*) not only to his own interests, but also to the interests of others. (1:29-30; 2:4)[11]

Consequently, the main thrust of the teaching is not that the Law is bad or negative and is to be rejected or left behind. Rather, what is to be left behind is boasting of the righteousness bestowed by the Law as of value in itself, before the end of one's life. A contemporary example would be giving value, let alone an absolute one, to being ahead by 20 or even 30 points at half-time in a basketball game. Paul's point here is not about God's law which, according to Paul, "is holy, and the commandment is holy and just and good" (Rom 7:12); it is about boasting of righteousness, which Paul refers to as "a righteousness of my own." This amounts to considering oneself the ultimate judge. It is precisely such an attitude which Paul strictly opposes in 1 Corinthians quoted above "lest after preaching to others I myself should be disqualified" (9:27), as well as earlier in that letter:

---

[11] Phil 2:4; 3:14, 17 account for all instances of the root *skop—* in this letter and they are all made in conjunction with a reference to the Roman stadium race.

This is how one should regard us, as servants of Christ and stewards of the mysteries of God. Moreover it is required of stewards that they be found trustworthy. But with me it is a very small thing that I should be judged by you or by any human court. I do not even judge myself. I am not aware of anything against myself, but I am not thereby acquitted. It is the Lord who judges me. Therefore do not pronounce judgment before the time, before the Lord comes, who will bring to light the things now hidden in darkness and will disclose the purposes of the heart. Then every man will receive his commendation from God. (4:1-5)

It is telling that a few verses later Paul uses irony to put to shame the Corinthians who think they have it made (Already you are filled! Already you have become rich! Without us you have become kings! And would that you did reign, so that we might share the rule with you! [v.8]) while he, the apostle, is still struggling in a kind of Roman arena, the "theater," where deadly games take place against gladiators and ferocious beasts: "For I think that God has exhibited us apostles as last of all, like men sentenced to death; because we have become a spectacle (*theatron*)[12] to the world, to angels and to men." (v.9)

From the above it ensues that Paul is not pitting Christ or grace against the Law, or even an actual "now" against an actual "then, earlier." Rather, he is referring to his personal "now" against the end of the road, which will not happen until Christ is revealed in God's glory. Until then, everything, including every "now," has no ultimate value of any sort. Until then, every presumed *accomplishment* on our part is to be thrown behind us until God has *accomplished* his work in us (Phil 1:6). In other words, if the Philippians are the true "circumcision," then they

---

[12] This is in contradistinction to the "amphitheater," an open theater, where literary plays were presented.

are bound by the new Law, that of Christ (Gal 6:2) and the Spirit of life (Rom 8:2) and thus are bound to walk *on the remainder of the road from the point at which they are*, according to the command of that Spirit (Gal 5:16, 25; Phil 2:1; 3:3) and not according to their own desires (Gal 5:17; Phil 3:3-4). Again, Paul is not arguing against the Law; rather, he is arguing against boasting in one's (accomplishments of the) flesh. Logically, this is the only possible way that Paul, the Jew, could give himself as an example to be followed by the Gentile Philippians. Notice, indeed, how at this juncture, he uses thrice in a row the same verb "count" (consider; *hēgoumai*) which he used earlier (Phil 3:3 and 6) when he invited the Philippians to follow the example of the Jewish Messiah: "But whatever gain I had, I *counted* (*hēgēmai*) as loss for the sake of Christ. Indeed I count (*hēgoumai*) everything as loss because of the surpassing worth of knowing Christ Jesus my Lord. For his sake I have suffered the loss of all things, and count (*hēgoumai*) them as refuse, in order that I may gain Christ." (Phil 3:7-8) Just as Christ threw behind himself whatever appeared to be his "own" and did not cling to it as an *harpagmon* (something to hold tight to) (2:6) but decided to receive it as "gift" from God, so also here Paul throws behind him his own apparent "blamelessness" and decides to look ahead (*skopon*), just as the runner would, for the "prize" from God (3:14). (Do you not know that in a race all the runners compete, but only one receives the prize? 1 Cor 9:24).[13] Notice,

---

[13] These are the only two instances of "prize" (*brabeion*) in the New Testament. The last instance of the root *brab*— occurs in Col 3:15 where the terminology parallels that of Philippians: "And above all these put on love, which binds everything together in *perfect* harmony. And let the peace of Christ rule (be ruled as a prize [by an umpire, a sporting event judge]; *brabevetō*) in your hearts, to which indeed you were *called* in the one body" (Col 3:14-15); "Not that I have already obtained this or *am already perfect*; but I press on to make it my own, because Christ Jesus has made me his own ... I

furthermore, that the passage concerning the "prize' in Philippians is introduced with the verb "consider" (Brethren, I do not consider (*logizomai*) that I have made it my own; but one thing I do, forgetting what lies behind and straining forward to what lies ahead; 3:13) that has the same meaning as "count" (*hēgoumai*). This is the same verb that Paul uses to speak of the "change" that is supposed to take place when one is "under (the) grace (of the law of the Spirit of life)" (Rom 6:14-15): "So you also must *consider* yourselves dead to sin and alive to God in Christ Jesus." (v.11) In Philippians, it is the verb "count" that allows both the Jewish Messiah and the Jewish Paul to be accounted as examples for the Gentile Philippians. In Romans, it is the parallel verb "consider" (reckon; *logizomai*) that allows Abraham the "Jew" to be an example for the Gentile Romans. Indeed, the lengthy discussion of the scriptural Abraham in Romans 4, which serves as a basis for that of Romans 6 concerning the new life to be led by the Gentiles, is replete with 11 occurrences of that verb and culminates with the following statement:

> That is why his faith was "reckoned to him as righteousness (*dikaiosynēn*)." But the words, "it was reckoned to him," *were written not for his sake alone, but for ours also.* It will be reckoned to us who believe in him that raised from the dead Jesus our Lord, who was put to death for our trespasses and raised for our justification (*dikaiōsin*). (Rom 6:22-24)

 The parallelism of Romans with Philippians is through the reference to righteousness as well as to the death and raising of Christ used in conjunction with making a Jew the example for the Gentiles to follow.

---

press on toward the goal for the *prize* of the upward *call* of God in Christ Jesus. Let those of us who are *perfect* be thus minded." (Phil 3:12, 14)

Thus the meaning and intention of Philippians 3:1-16 is clear. Whenever Paul would concentrate on his own accomplishments, he would miss the mark, not because the Law is "inferior" to the grace brought about through Christ, but because he would be emitting a verdict of "blamelessness," and thus "righteousness," on himself. In so doing, he would be erring doubly: by acting as the judge and by pronouncing judgment in an untimely manner, before the end of the course. He would be misreading scripture which witnesses to the fact that righteousness comes through God's emissary, who was absolutely obedient even until his last breath and without ever opening his mouth, let alone declaring his own righteousness.[14] It is then only by following the example of Christ that Paul would eventually accede to the glory that was granted to Christ at the end of his course, should he, Paul, continue until the end of his own course on the path of blamelessness that he has secured until now. Indeed, it is being able to "conform (*symmorphozomenos*) to the (obedient) death of Christ" (3:10) that he would have a chance that "his lowly body" at the resurrection from the dead (v.11) be "conform (*symmorphon*) to the glorious body of Christ" (v.21).

Actually, it was by submitting to the message of Second-Isaiah that Paul discovered that it is only according to his own assessment that he is righteous. How could one be righteous while persecuting and dismantling the "congregation" (*ekklēsian, qahal*), the handiwork of God himself?[15] That this thought was on Paul's mind in this passage is evident from his use of the verb *diōkō*, which allows a wordplay since it means "pursue" and by extension "persecute" (pursue with the intention of harming):

---

[14] See Rom 3:21-22.
[15] See Gal 1:13, 23.

And I myself have reason for confidence in the flesh also. If any other man thinks he has reason for confidence in the flesh, I have more: circumcised on the eighth day, of the people of Israel, of the tribe of Benjamin, a Hebrew born of Hebrews; as to the law a Pharisee, as to zeal a persecutor (*diōkōn*) of the church, as to righteousness under the law blameless. But whatever gain I had, I counted as loss for the sake of Christ ... Not that I have already obtained this or am already perfect; but I press on (pursue; *diōkō*) to make it my own, because Christ Jesus has made me his own. Brethren, I do not consider that I have made it my own; but one thing I do, forgetting what lies behind and straining forward to what lies ahead, I press on (pursue; *diōkō*) toward the goal for the prize of the upward call of God in Christ Jesus. (3:4-7, 12-14)

From having been a "persecutor" and dismantler of God's "congregation" he turns into someone who pursues the goal "of the upward call of God in Christ Jesus" without ever assuming that he attained it. Paul acknowledges the evident: how could he attain the end before the end? He realized that, whatever his prominence, he is after all a member of God's congregation and not the judge, for to be judge is tantamount to being God. At the most he could be only another Moses. To go beyond Moses, the disobedient servant, Paul must follow in the footsteps of the Isaianic obedient servant, God's Christ and ultimate emissary. And this is precisely what he is asking the Philippians to do.

Since Christ's "lordship" will not be revealed openly to the world until his coming (3:20-21), so also will his vindication by God as *the righteous one.* It is at that time, and only then, that everyone's righteousness will be measured against Christ's. This is precisely Isaiah's teaching:

Yet it was the will of the Lord to bruise him; he has put him to grief; when he makes himself an offering for sin, he shall see his offspring, he shall prolong his days; the will of the Lord shall prosper in his hand; he shall see the fruit of the travail of his soul and be satisfied; by his knowledge shall the righteous one, my servant, make many to be accounted righteous; and he shall bear their iniquities. (Is 53:10-11)

Consequently, Paul understood that the verdict on his own righteousness against the demands of the Law in the middle of the "way" (Phil 3:9) risked being overturned, since at any moment in the future he might fail. He thus opted to put his trust (faith) in the righteousness that comes from God, whose verdict was issued regarding Christ, God's obedient servant, who trusted in God's righteousness against all odds. Christ's trust in God is an invitation for the Philippians to follow suit by trusting both that God vindicated his Christ and that he will vindicate them to the extent to which they will have trusted in his promise and his verdict: "For his (Christ's) sake I have suffered the loss of all things, and count them as refuse, in order that I may gain Christ and be found in him, not having a righteousness of my own, based on law, but that which is through Christ's trust (in God),[16] the righteousness from God that depends on (my) trust." (vv.8-9) To have this trust, one is to follow Christ's example, as Paul did, and even suffer a shameful end (v.10) so that "*if possible (in some way) I may reach the resurrection (exanastasin)*, which is the one (*tēn*) from the dead" (v.11).

In order to properly understand this last verse and its function in Paul's argument, a digression is in order here. More often than not, in theological terminology, the difference between resurrection and life (eternal) has been eliminated in the same way as that between death and (death on the) cross.[17] This was done under the influence of (especially Platonic, then Plotinic)

---

[16] Or "through my trust in (what God did to and through) Christ."

[17] See my comments above on Phil 2:5-11.

philosophical terminology that pervaded theological discussions in Alexandrian and later Byzantine circles. Against the grain of scripture, the point of reference became the individual instead of the community: (individualistic) Christology gave birth to (individualistic) anthropology. The classical text with which one ought to begin (and end) discussion concerning the differentiation between resurrection and life (eternal) is a passage from the scriptural reading heard at Orthodox funeral services: "Do not marvel at this; for the hour is coming when all who are in the tombs will hear his voice and come forth, those who have done good, to the resurrection of life, and those who have done evil, to the resurrection of judgment." (Jn 5:28-29) It echoes what is written in the Book of Revelation:

> Then I saw a great white throne and him who sat upon it; from his presence earth and sky fled away, and no place was found for them. And I saw the dead, great and small, standing before the throne, and books were opened. Also another book was opened, which is the book of life. And the dead were judged by what was written in the books, by what they had done. And the sea gave up the dead in it, Death and Hades gave up the dead in them, and all were judged by what they had done. Then Death and Hades were thrown into the lake of fire. This is the second death, the lake of fire; and if any one's name was not found written in the book of life, he was thrown into the lake of fire. (Rev 20:11-15)

The reason then that resurrection must not be equated with life eternal is that the basic intent and function of raising the dead is to bring those who have died before the coming Lord for judgment. Judgment takes place only once, before the seat of God.[18]

Consequently, Paul's hope is to be raised unto life eternal should he be found righteous (Phil 3:9-11). This explains his use here of *exanastasin* (resurrection from, raising out of), unique in the New Testament, instead of the common *anastasin* (rising/arising).[19] The intent is to indicate that he will, hopefully, be counted among those who will be granted the life promised in the Law and not end up under the curse of death as punishment, the alternative spoken of in the same Law. Put otherwise, in contradistinction with *anastasin*, which is general and applies to all the dead, including Jesus Christ (1 Cor 15:13), *exanastasin* has the connotation of "standing out" and differentiates between the dead who will be raised to accede unto life eternal and those who will be raised to be relegated to the domain of death as punishment, that is, away from the company of the only living and life-giving God. This connotation of standing out of the similar surrounding is also found in the use of the verb *exanistēmi* (of the same root as the noun *exanastasin*) in the New Testament. The first instance occurs in the statement found in Mark and then taken up by Luke: "Teacher, Moses wrote for us that if a man's brother dies and leaves a wife, but leaves no child, the man must take the wife, and raise up (*exanastēsē*) children (seed; *sperma/progeny*) for his brother." (Mk 12:19/Lk 20:28) This case actually corresponds fully to what is intended in Philippians: despite the fact that the brother remains dead, his progeny nevertheless is brought out into the domain of life through *exanastasin*. The other instance describes the action of

---

[18] Here again the individual judgment upon death is not scriptural. It was introduced later under the influence of Platonism and its teaching regarding the immortality of the soul.

[19] See e.g. Acts 4:2; 17:32; 24:15; 1 Cor 15:12, 13, 22, 42.

some who emerged out of the surrounding company: "But some
believers who belonged to the party of the Pharisees rose up
(*exanestēsan*), and said, 'It is necessary to circumcise them, and to
charge them to keep the law of Moses.'" (Acts 15:5) This reading
is further corroborated by the only instance of the noun
exanastasin in the Septuagint: "For in seven days I will send rain
upon the earth forty days and forty nights; and *every living thing*
(*pasan tēn exanastasin*-everything that was brought about) that I
have made I will blot out from the face of the ground." (Gen
7:4) *Exanastasin* here is the translation of the Hebrew *yequm*
(something which is raised [above, out of the surrounding]) and
fits the context where every living thing that had been brought
up out of the level ground by God was about to be erased and
brought back to its origin: level ground.

In the following verses (Phil 3:12-14) Paul proceeds to show
how his hoped for *exanastasin* will happen, in preparation for the
inclusion of the Philippians in this hope (vv.15-16). He appeals
to the imagery of the Roman race. In Paul's race, the goal is the
finish line where the vindicated Christ is already waiting for his
companions. Christ, who was the first and thus had no one to
emulate, had to be the person of total trust as the Isaianic Lord's
servant was expected to be. On the other hand, the racing
believers, including Paul, who have Christ as the example before
them, have an extra reason not to put their trust in their
accomplishments. It is more secure, safe, assured (*asphales*; v.1)
for them to keep looking toward the goal and to put their trust
in God and his Christ, who has already reached that goal. That is
to say, they are to keep being drawn by (God through the
example of his) Christ toward that goal: "Not that I have already
obtained (*elabon*) this or am already perfect; but I press on to
obtain (*katalabō*) it, since I am surely being pulled ahead
(obtained, received; *katelēmphthēn*) by Christ Jesus. Brethren, I

do not consider that I have already obtained (reached [the goal]; *kateilēphenai*)." (vv.12-13a) The entire statement is built as wordplay around the root (*kata*)*lamb*— meaning to grasp, hold, attain, thus also to receive. This translation, in which the aorist *katelēmphthēn* is understood as an expression of assuredness rather than of realization as reflected in the perfect *kateilēphenai*, is borne out by the following: "but one thing I do, forgetting what lies behind and straining forward to what lies ahead, I press on toward the goal for the prize of the upward call of God in Christ Jesus." (vv.13b-14) This "ahead-ness," rather than a static, mystical "above-ness," of Jesus Christ is corroborated in what Paul will write a few verses later: "But our commonwealth is in heaven,[20] and from it *we await expectantly* a Savior, the Lord Jesus Christ" (v.20) who is the "coming," rather than the "descending," Lord.

What are the Philippians to do? If they want to be perfect (mature; *teleioi*) they ought to think accordingly (*touto phronōmen*; v.15), that is, to follow the lead of Paul, who realized "not that I am already perfect (*teteleiōmai*)" (v.12). One can imagine how the following phrase "and if in anything you think (*phroneite*) otherwise, God will reveal that also to you" (v.15) could be—and has been—misconstrued by later philosophical theology, which viewed this passage in terms of a continual mental revelation of the expression and meaning of the true and correct understanding and formulation of the "faith,"—a revelation imparted especially to the (true) "theologians." Such an understanding must be discounted for the following reasons.

First and foremost, although the Greek verb *phroneō* means "think" and is linked essentially to mental cogitation, it is used in

---

[20] In scripture, heaven is not so much a place above as it is the domain of God.

Pauline literature in parallel with the scriptural *peripateō* "walk" (on the way prescribed by the Law; according to God's will). This is Paul's way to include the Gentiles with Jews under the authority and rule of God, as their new paterfamilias, and to invite them to abide under that rule and authority. He uses his famous doubling "abba, the father" in Galatians (4:6) to underscore that "in Christ Jesus you are *all* sons of God ... There is neither Jew nor Greek ... for you are *all* one in Christ Jesus" (3:26, 28).[21] Later, in that letter, we find the same "doubling" between 'think" and "walk": "I have confidence in the Lord that you will not think anything other(wise)[22] ... But I say, walk by the Spirit, and do not gratify the desires of the flesh." (5:10, 16) The intended parallelism between these two verbs—as well as between mind and behavior—is at its clearest in the classic text in Romans (which parallels what we hear in Galatians) that requires all, including the freed Gentiles, to abide by the law of the Spirit, which grants continual life along the lines of the Law in Deuteronomy:

There is therefore now no condemnation for those who are in Christ Jesus. For the law of the Spirit of life in Christ Jesus has set me free from the law of sin and death. For God has done what the law, weakened by the flesh, could not do: sending his own Son in the likeness of sinful flesh and for sin, he condemned sin in the flesh, in order that the just requirement of the law might be fulfilled in us, who *walk* (*peripatousin*) not according to the flesh but according to the Spirit. For those who are according to the flesh *think* (*phronousin*) the matters of the flesh, but those who (are) according to the Spirit (*think* [*phronousin*]) the matters of the Spirit. The thought (thinking; *phronēma*) of the flesh is death, but

---

[21] See my comments in *Gal* 165-85.
[22] This statement approximates closely Phil 3:15 (Let those of us who are mature [perfect] think accordingly).

the thought (thinking; *phronēma*) of the Spirit is life and peace. *For the thought (thinking;* phronēma*) of the flesh is hostile to God; it does not submit (*hypotassetai*) to God's law, indeed it cannot; and those who are in the flesh cannot please God ... So then, brethren, we are debtors, not to the flesh, to *live* according to the flesh—for if you *live* according to the flesh you will die, but if by the Spirit you put to death the *deeds* of the body you will *live*. For as many as are led (*agontai*) by the Spirit of God[23] are sons of God.* (Romans 8:1-8, 12-14)

Paul's Deuteronomic approach is unmistakable. He is trying to draw the Gentiles away from cogitating assumedly correctly, à la Adam, to behaving correctly according to God's will, by submitting (subordinating) their "thinking" (*phronēma*) to God's law.

This understanding is further corroborated by the fact that when speaking to the Philippians he starts with "think" but ends with *stoikhein* (walk in line [under someone's directive, as in the army]). This is precisely the verb he uses in Galatians at the end of the passage in which he invites the Galatians to "walk" according to the Spirit, and not the flesh: "But I say, walk (*peripateite*) by the Spirit, and do not gratify the desires of the flesh ... If we live by the Spirit, let us also walk (*stoikhōmen*) by the Spirit." (Gal 5:16, 25)

However, in Galatians, the Spirit is not a self-standing entity, let alone a free agent, roaming around and waiting to "descend on" and "abide in" the "perfect" or "spiritual." The Spirit's reality is always and continually bound to Paul's words of instruction. It was imparted to them through "the word of preaching that they have heard (*akoēs*)" and to which they have

---

[23] Compare with Gal 5:18 (But if you are led [*agesthe*] by the Spirit).

trustingly (*pisteōs*) submitted (Gal 3:2, 5). Thus, the Spirit is not "possessed" by the believers; rather it is to be submitted to, in total obedience (*stoikhein*). Time and again, the Galatians faltered from its directive, so much so that the Apostle continued to be "in travail until Christ be formed in you!" (4:19). And since he cannot be with them forever, he is committing the Spirit in "writing" (1:8-9; 5:2-3), in a letter sealed with his hand (6:11), that would be continually "read" to them in order for them to perpetually "hear" the "voice of the Apostle" (5:20) and, in so doing, receive time and again the Spirit first hand and thus unadulterated by their own "thoughts":

> I feel a divine jealousy for you, for I betrothed you to Christ to present you as a pure bride to her one husband. But I am afraid that as the serpent deceived Eve by his cunning, your thoughts (*noēmata*; from the same root as *nous* [mind]) will be led astray from a sincere and pure devotion to Christ. For if some one comes and preaches *another Jesus* than the one we preached, or if you receive *a different spirit* from the one you received, or if you accept *a different gospel* from the one you accepted, you submit to it readily enough. (2 Cor 11:2-4)

Notice here that the community has not yet been perfected as the bride of the coming Christ and needs to be continually "cleansed with the word" (Eph 5:26) in order to be finally subordinated to Christ (v.22), since to him everything shall be subordinated (Phil 3:21; see also 1 Cor 15:27-28).

If the Philippians are required to continue "staying in line" (*stoikhein*) no matter at what point they are in the race (Phil 3:16), then the phrase "and if in anything you are otherwise minded, God will reveal that also to you" (v.15b) cannot possibly mean that the believers will be individually privy to a special "revelation" by God that would guide them further.

Such a "revelation" would not be possible since it would contradict the original apostolic teaching received through revelation (Gal 1:12, 16). Also, notice how God's "revelation" referred to in Philippians has a negative function rather than a positive one: it is intended to preserve the Philippians from falling away into thinking "something other" (*ti heterōs*; 3:15b). In other words, it amounts to letting them know that they should proceed on the path already trodden, which is precisely what v.16 is saying: "Only let us hold true to what we have attained." The writer is doing here precisely what Paul did in Galatians by consigning in writing once and for all the "revelation" he is referring to, and he is assumedly sending it with Epaphroditus, whom Paul introduced as his alter ego (2:15). It is at the hearing of this epistle, time and again, that the Philippians will be led to proceed on the safe path. Thus, the so-called "tradition" of reading the Apostle's letters to all the churches was actually *imposed* by the Pauline school. This is clear from what we hear in Colossians: "And when this letter has been read among you, have it read also in the church of the Laodiceans; and see that you read also the letter from Laodicea." (4:16) Any further divine "revelation" comes from the Pauline text that carries the Apostle's original teaching throughout the ages. Any other thought is from Satan:

> And what I do I will continue to do, in order to undermine the claim of those who would like to claim that in their boasted mission they work on the same terms as we do. For such men are false apostles, deceitful workmen, disguising themselves as apostles of Christ. And no wonder, for even Satan disguises himself as an angel of light. So it is not strange if his servants also disguise themselves as servants of righteousness. Their end will correspond to their deeds. (2 Cor 11:12-15)

Now concerning the coming of our Lord Jesus Christ and our assembling to meet him, we beg you, brethren, not to be quickly shaken in mind or excited, either by spirit or by word, or by letter purporting to be from us, to the effect that the day of the Lord has come. Let no one deceive you in any way ... So then, brethren, stand firm and hold to the traditions which you were taught by us, either by word of mouth or by letter. (2 Thess 2:1-3, 15)

Vv. 17-21 ¹⁷Συμμιμηταί μου γίνεσθε, ἀδελφοί, καὶ σκοπεῖτε τοὺς οὕτω περιπατοῦντας καθὼς ἔχετε τύπον ἡμᾶς. ¹⁸πολλοὶ γὰρ περιπατοῦσιν οὓς πολλάκις ἔλεγον ὑμῖν, νῦν δὲ καὶ κλαίων λέγω, τοὺς ἐχθροὺς τοῦ σταυροῦ τοῦ Χριστοῦ, ¹⁹ὧν τὸ τέλος ἀπώλεια, ὧν ὁ θεὸς ἡ κοιλία καὶ ἡ δόξα ἐν τῇ αἰσχύνῃ αὐτῶν, οἱ τὰ ἐπίγεια φρονοῦντες. ²⁰ἡμῶν γὰρ τὸ πολίτευμα ἐν οὐρανοῖς ὑπάρχει, ἐξ οὗ καὶ σωτῆρα ἀπεκδεχόμεθα κύριον Ἰησοῦν Χριστόν, ²¹ὃς μετασχηματίσει τὸ σῶμα τῆς ταπεινώσεως ἡμῶν σύμμορφον τῷ σώματι τῆς δόξης αὐτοῦ κατὰ τὴν ἐνέργειαν τοῦ δύνασθαι αὐτὸν καὶ ὑποτάξαι αὐτῷ τὰ πάντα.

¹⁷Brethren, join in imitating me, and mark those who so live as you have an example in us. ¹⁸For many, of whom I have often told you and now tell you even with tears, live as enemies of the cross of Christ. ¹⁹Their end is destruction, their god is the belly, and they glory in their shame, with minds set on earthly things. ²⁰But our commonwealth is in heaven, and from it we await a Savior, the Lord Jesus Christ, ²¹who will change our lowly body to be like his glorious body, by the power which enables him even to subject all things to himself.

While giving himself as an example to be followed Paul uses the verb "walk" as well as *skopeite* (mark; keep within your vision), which is from the same root as the noun *skopon* (goal) he used a few verses earlier: "I pursue [my path] according (press on toward; *diokō*) the goal" (Phil 3:14). The alternative is to walk a different path, which corresponds to "thinking (*phroneite*) differently" (v.15) and "thinking (with minds set on; *phronountes*) the earthly matters" (v.18), that is, unlike "citizens of the heavens" (v.20). Again, the connection to Galatians can be seen not only in the mention of "shame" (Phil 3:19), which is the opposite of boasting (Gal 6:12-14), but also in the expression "the cross of Christ" (Phil 3:18; Gal 6:12).[24] This phrase, found elsewhere in the New Testament only in 1 Corinthians 1:17, is a clear reference to Paul's preaching (vv.17-23). Consequently, beyond Paul's *behavior* it is actually his *teaching as to how one is to behave*, which is of essence. This is corroborated in 1 Corinthians where the Apostle writes:

> For though you have countless guides in Christ, you do not have many fathers. For I became your father in Christ Jesus through the gospel. I urge you, then, be imitators of me. Therefore I sent to you Timothy, my beloved and faithful child in the Lord, to remind you of *my ways* in Christ, *as I teach them everywhere in every church.* (4:15-17)

The last two verses (Phil 3:20-21) put the seal on the fact that the Pauline imagery is Roman through and through. They speak of the believers' eventual vindication in terms of a Roman general who, having won the war against enemies that were subjugating his co-citizens, is coming to liberate his fellow citizens. Liberation is assured through the leader's victory. It is only a matter of time before Paul's co-citizens will be granted liberty so long as they remain faithful by "holding true to what they have attained" (v.16), that is to say, "provided we suffer with him in order that we may also be glorified with him" (Rom

---

[24] In Gal 6:14 we have "the cross of our Lord Jesus Christ."

8:17).[25] The victory for the Roman general and his co-citizens is sealed at the pompous procession granted by the emperor in Rome:

> But our commonwealth is in heaven, and from it we await a Savior, the Lord Jesus Christ, who will change our lowly body to be like his glorious body, by the power which enables him even to subject all things to himself. (Phil 3:20-21)

> But each in his own order: Christ the first fruits, then at his coming those who belong to Christ. Then comes the end, when he delivers the kingdom to God the Father after destroying every rule and every authority and power. For he must reign until he has put all his enemies under his feet. The last enemy to be destroyed is death. "For God has put all things in subjection under his feet." But when it says, "All things are put in subjection under him," it is plain that he is excepted who put all things under him. When all things are subjected to him, then the Son himself will also be subjected to him who put all things under him, that God may be everything to every one. (1 Cor 15:23-28)

Thus, the glory already granted to Jesus Christ (Phil 2:9-11) is promised to his co-citizens in the Kingdom that is coming only if they continue to behave in obedience to God's commandments and do his will. This behavior specifically means caring for every needy *'adam* (human being), and not, as was made of it later during the theologico-philosophical debates, in "confessing in words the correct formula of faith":[26]

> You will know them by their fruits. Are grapes gathered from thorns, or figs from thistles? So, every sound tree bears good fruit,

---

[25] See also earlier in Philippians: "that I may know him and the power of his resurrection, and may share his sufferings, becoming like him in his death, that if possible I may attain the resurrection from the dead." (3:10-11)

[26] Let alone the endless discussions as how our glorified body will look like!

but the bad tree bears evil fruit. A sound tree cannot bear evil fruit, nor can a bad tree bear good fruit. Every tree that does not bear good fruit is cut down and thrown into the fire. Thus you will know them by their fruits. Not every one who says to me, "Lord, Lord," shall enter the kingdom of heaven, but he who does the will of my Father who is in heaven. On that day many will say to me, "Lord, Lord, did we not prophesy in your name, and cast out demons in your name, and do many mighty works in your name?" And then will I declare to them, "I never knew you; depart from me, you evildoers." Every one then who hears these words of mine and does them will be like a wise man who built his house upon the rock; and the rain fell, and the floods came, and the winds blew and beat upon that house, but it did not fall, because it had been founded on the rock. And every one who hears these words of mine and does not do them will be like a foolish man who built his house upon the sand; and the rain fell, and the floods came, and the winds blew and beat against that house, and it fell; and great was the fall of it. (Mt 7:16-27)

Chapter 4

Vv. 1-9 ¹ Ὥστε, ἀδελφοί μου ἀγαπητοὶ καὶ ἐπιπόθητοι, χαρὰ καὶ στέφανός μου, οὕτως στήκετε ἐν κυρίῳ, ἀγαπητοί. ²Εὐοδίαν παρακαλῶ καὶ Συντύχην παρακαλῶ τὸ αὐτὸ φρονεῖν ἐν κυρίῳ. ³ναὶ ἐρωτῶ καὶ σέ, γνήσιε σύζυγε, συλλαμβάνου αὐταῖς, αἵτινες ἐν τῷ εὐαγγελίῳ συνήθλησάν μοι μετὰ καὶ Κλήμεντος καὶ τῶν λοιπῶν συνεργῶν μου, ὧν τὰ ὀνόματα ἐν βίβλῳ ζωῆς. ⁴Χαίρετε ἐν κυρίῳ πάντοτε· πάλιν ἐρῶ, χαίρετε. ⁵τὸ ἐπιεικὲς ὑμῶν γνωσθήτω πᾶσιν ἀνθρώποις. ὁ κύριος ἐγγύς. ⁶μηδὲν μεριμνᾶτε, ἀλλ᾽ ἐν παντὶ τῇ προσευχῇ καὶ τῇ δεήσει μετὰ εὐχαριστίας τὰ αἰτήματα ὑμῶν γνωριζέσθω πρὸς τὸν θεόν. ⁷καὶ ἡ εἰρήνη τοῦ θεοῦ ἡ ὑπερέχουσα πάντα νοῦν φρουρήσει τὰς καρδίας ὑμῶν καὶ τὰ νοήματα ὑμῶν ἐν Χριστῷ Ἰησοῦ. ⁸Τὸ λοιπόν, ἀδελφοί, ὅσα ἐστὶν ἀληθῆ, ὅσα σεμνά, ὅσα δίκαια, ὅσα ἁγνά, ὅσα προσφιλῆ, ὅσα εὔφημα, εἴ τις ἀρετὴ καὶ εἴ τις ἔπαινος, ταῦτα λογίζεσθε· ⁹ἃ καὶ ἐμάθετε καὶ παρελάβετε καὶ ἠκούσατε καὶ εἴδετε ἐν ἐμοί, ταῦτα πράσσετε· καὶ ὁ θεὸς τῆς εἰρήνης ἔσται μεθ᾽ ὑμῶν.

¹Therefore, my brethren, whom I love and long for, my joy and crown, stand firm thus in the Lord, my beloved. ²I entreat Euodia and I entreat Syntyche to agree in the Lord. ³And I ask you also, true yokefellow, help these women, for they have labored side by side with me in the gospel together with Clement and the rest of my fellow workers, whose names are in the book of life. ⁴Rejoice in the Lord always; again I will say, Rejoice. ⁵Let all men know your forbearance. The Lord is at hand. ⁶Have no anxiety about anything, but in everything by prayer and supplication with thanksgiving let your requests be made known to God. ⁷ And the peace of God, which passes all understanding, will keep your hearts and your minds in Christ Jesus. ⁸Finally, brethren, whatever is true, whatever is honorable, whatever is

just, whatever is pure, whatever is lovely, whatever is gracious, if
there is any excellence, if there is anything worthy of praise,
think about these things. ⁹What you have learned and received
and heard and seen in me, do; and the God of peace will be
with you.

In this passage we have the only other use of the conjunction
hōste (therefore), which has the connotation of a final
conclusion. Just as earlier the passage that speaks of Christ's
glorification (Phil 2:6-11) ends with an *hōste* (therefore)
requiring the Philippians to continue in their obedience (vv.12-
13), the other passage referring to the Lord's glory (3:20-21)
ends with a request that they "stand firm in the Lord." The link
between the two pericopes is enhanced through the use of
"beloved" in the address in both cases (2:12 and 4:1). Given that
the latter request is made in conjunction with the Lord's coming,
the Apostle calls them "my joy and crown." The other instance
of this terminology in the New Testament occurs in a similar
setting: "For what is *our* hope or *joy or crown* of boasting before
our Lord Jesus at his coming? Is it not you? For you are our glory
and joy." (1 Thess 2:19-20) This "looking ahead" (Phil 3:20) is
linked to the fact that the Apostle seems sure that he will never
see the Philippians again, except in the Kingdom, which in turn
betrays the fact that he may already be dead. Indeed, the author
prepares the hearers for this possibility through the use of
epipotheō (yearn for, long for) in the following sequence.
Between the yearning for the Philippians through Christ for
whose cause Paul is in jail (1:8) and in conjunction with Christ's
coming (4:1), we have the longing for them that the Apostle

plans to satisfy through the sending of Epaphroditus, his alter ego (3:25-26).[1]

In Galatians, the test for true understanding of the gospel (Gal 2:1-10) was not an intellectual pursuit, but rather a practical one: full table fellowship (2:11-14), a test which Peter and Barnabas failed miserably. It is no wonder then that Paul dedicated lengthy passages to this matter in Romans (14:1-15:6) and 1 Corinthians (8; 10:14-11:1; 11:17-34). It makes also sense that he would revisit the matter in Philippians. The names Evodia and Syntyche in Philippians 4:2 refer to the Jews on the one hand, and to the Gentiles, on the other hand. *Ev-(h)odia* is the one who follows correctly and faithfully (*ev*—) the path (*hodos*), that is, the Jews who "walk" by Paul's "rule" (*kanōn*) and are the "Israel of God" (Gal 6:16). It follows that *Syn-tykhe* would then be those Gentiles who have joined through *tykhe* (good fate and thus "sheer grace") with (*syn*—) the "Israel of God" and thus became one with it through grafting as Paul explains in Romans 11. Therefore, Paul is inviting the Jews and Gentiles of Philippi to "think the same thing (in the same manner)," that is, to behave in a manner that shows their unity: sharing fully in the same table fellowship. The reference to oneness in behavior rather than in a formulaic expression of belief is further corroborated by the similar phraseology: "stand firm (*stēkete*) in the Lord ... they have strived side by side (*synēthlēsan*) with me in the gospel" (Phil 4:1, 3), and "Only let your manner of life be worthy of the gospel of Christ, so that ... I may hear of you that you stand firm (*stēkete*) in one spirit, with one mind striving side by side (*synathlountes*) for the faith of the gospel" (1:27).

---

[1] See earlier my comments on these verses.

The "true (*gnēsie*; genuine) yokefellow" who is to "hold them together by the hand" (*syllambanou avtais*) is none other than Timothy, Paul's heir. Timothy was a Jew who had to be circumcised by Paul (Acts 16:1-3) and thus his fellow under the yoke of the Law. Earlier he was spoken of as the sole "child" (*teknon*; Phil 2:22) "who will be genuinely (*gnēsiōs*) anxious for your welfare" (2:20)[2] In this mission Timothy will have the help of God, the "Clement (Merciful)" one[3] and the other "fellow-workers" of Paul, whose names, the Apostle hopes, are in the Book of Life on the grounds that they are partakers of the gospel and thus will be with him wherever Christ is (1:22-23). With this thought in mind Paul insistently asks the Philippians to rejoice (*Rejoice* in the Lord always; again I will say, *Rejoice*; 4:4) as he himself did earlier (I *rejoice*. Yes, and I *shall rejoice*; 1:18-19). And since the Lord is at hand, the path toward the end is shorter than it was at the beginning as Paul explains in Romans 13:11-12. Therefore, the Philippians are to concentrate on the one thing necessary: "forbearance" (*epieikes*) toward all men (Phil 4:5). This forbearance requires love for the neighbor. Indeed, in another Pauline letter (2 Cor 10:1) the same forbearance (*epieikias*; gentleness) is coupled with meekness (*prautētos*; gentleness), which is also the quality required in dealing with the "weaker brother" in Galatians 6:1, and is a facet of love, the fruit of the Spirit (5:22-23),[4] that is opposed to works of the flesh (vv.17a, 19-21). The Philippians are not to worry about

---

[2] Elsewhere he is addressed by Paul as "true child" (*gnēsiō teknō*) in 1 Tim 1:2.

[3] The Latin *clemens* corresponds to the Greek *oiktirmōn*, the one who is full of mercies (*oiktirmoi*; Phil 2:1; see above my comment on this verse). A similar instance is found in Col 4:10-11 where, among Paul's Jewish helpers, we hear of Aristarchus, Mark, and Jesus who is called Justus. Clearly, the Latin *justus* is the translation of the Greek *dikaios* (righteous). Thus, this Jesus is none other than Jesus Christ, the "righteous one."

[4] See my comments on these verses in *Gal* 297-301.

anything else. To the contrary, they are to make known to God their requests while thanking him (Phil 4:6) "for your Father knows what you need before you ask him" (Mt 6:8) and look ahead toward the peace of his kingdom (Phil 4:7), which peace is the end of the path he started them on through his grace (1:2).

Besides the specific requirement of love toward all men, which is at the heart of the gospel, <u>the Philippians ought to behave as any decent Roman citizen, including Paul (4:9a) himself a Roman citizen, would behave (4:8)</u>. After all, Rome is interested in establishing the *pax Romana* (the Roman peace) throughout the empire. All <u>"Roman" believers, including the Philippians, themselves descendents of Roman soldiers, should oblige, given</u> that their God is "the God of peace" who "protects" as a mighty army would (*phrourēsei*).[5] Indeed, the close link between Paul's requests that they "behave as citizens" (*politevesthe*; 1:27) and "live at peace" (*eirēnevete*) is clear from the parallel texts of 2 Corinthians and Romans:

> I entreat (*parakalō*) Euodia and I entreat (*parakalō*) Syntyche to agree (*to avto phronein*) in the Lord ... *Rejoice* in the Lord always ... *Finally, brethren*, whatever is true, whatever is honorable, whatever is just, whatever is pure, whatever is lovely, whatever is gracious, if there is any excellence, if there is anything worthy of praise, think about these things ... *and the God of peace will be with you.* (Phil 4:1, 4, 8, 9)

> *Finally, brethren, rejoice.* Mend your ways, heed my appeal (*parakaleisthe*), agree with one another (*to avto phroneite*), live in peace (*eirēnevete*), and *the God of love and peace will be with you.* (2 Cor 13:11)

---

[5] The verb *phroureō* used in Phil 4:7 has the connotation of guarding someone tightly as in a "jail" or under "house arrest," and is a military term.

Live in harmony (*to avto phronountes*) with one another ... If possible, so far as it depends upon you, live peaceably (*eirēnevontes*) with all. (Rom 12:16, 18)

Vv. 10-20 ¹⁰Ἐχάρην δὲ ἐν κυρίῳ μεγάλως ὅτι ἤδη ποτὲ ἀνεθάλετε τὸ ὑπὲρ ἐμοῦ φρονεῖν, ἐφ' ᾧ καὶ ἐφρονεῖτε, ἠκαιρεῖσθε δέ. ¹¹οὐχ ὅτι καθ' ὑστέρησιν λέγω, ἐγὼ γὰρ ἔμαθον ἐν οἷς εἰμι αὐτάρκης εἶναι. ¹²οἶδα καὶ ταπεινοῦσθαι, οἶδα καὶ περισσεύειν· ἐν παντὶ καὶ ἐν πᾶσιν μεμύημαι, καὶ χορτάζεσθαι καὶ πεινᾶν καὶ περισσεύειν καὶ ὑστερεῖσθαι· ¹³πάντα ἰσχύω ἐν τῷ ἐνδυναμοῦντί με. ¹⁴πλὴν καλῶς ἐποιήσατε συγκοινωνήσαντές μου τῇ θλίψει. ¹⁵οἴδατε δὲ καὶ ὑμεῖς, Φιλιππήσιοι, ὅτι ἐν ἀρχῇ τοῦ εὐαγγελίου, ὅτε ἐξῆλθον ἀπὸ Μακεδονίας, οὐδεμία μοι ἐκκλησία ἐκοινώνησεν εἰς λόγον δόσεως καὶ λήμψεως εἰ μὴ ὑμεῖς μόνοι, ¹⁶ὅτι καὶ ἐν Θεσσαλονίκῃ καὶ ἅπαξ καὶ δὶς εἰς τὴν χρείαν μοι ἐπέμψατε. ¹⁷οὐχ ὅτι ἐπιζητῶ τὸ δόμα, ἀλλὰ ἐπιζητῶ τὸν καρπὸν τὸν πλεονάζοντα εἰς λόγον ὑμῶν. ¹⁸ἀπέχω δὲ πάντα καὶ περισσεύω· πεπλήρωμαι δεξάμενος παρὰ Ἐπαφροδίτου τὰ παρ' ὑμῶν, ὀσμὴν εὐωδίας, θυσίαν δεκτήν, εὐάρεστον τῷ θεῷ. ¹⁹ὁ δὲ θεός μου πληρώσει πᾶσαν χρείαν ὑμῶν κατὰ τὸ πλοῦτος αὐτοῦ ἐν δόξῃ ἐν Χριστῷ Ἰησοῦ. ²⁰τῷ δὲ θεῷ καὶ πατρὶ ἡμῶν ἡ δόξα εἰς τοὺς αἰῶνας τῶν αἰώνων, ἀμήν.

¹⁰I rejoice in the Lord greatly that now at length you have revived your concern for me; you were indeed concerned for me, but you had no opportunity. ¹¹Not that I complain of want; for I have learned, in whatever state I am, to be content. ¹²I know how to be abased, and I know how to abound; in any and all circumstances I have learned the secret of facing plenty and hunger, abundance and want. ¹³I can do all things in him who strengthens me. ¹⁴Yet it was kind of you to share my trouble. ¹⁵And you Philippians yourselves know that in the beginning of the gospel, when I left Macedonia, no church entered into partnership with me in giving and receiving except you only;

¹⁶for even in Thessalonica you sent me help once and again. ¹⁷Not that I seek the gift; but I seek the fruit which increases to your credit. ¹⁸I have received full payment, and more; I am filled, having received from Epaphroditus the gifts you sent, a fragrant offering, a sacrifice acceptable and pleasing to God. ¹⁹And my God will supply every need of yours according to his riches in glory in Christ Jesus. ²⁰To our God and Father be glory for ever and ever. Amen.

This passage (Phil 4:10-20) forms an *inclusio* with the opening passage (1:3-11) and announces the close of the letter. Paul congratulates the Philippians on their sharing with him in the gospel (*synkoinōnēsantes* 4:14; *ekoinōnēsen* 4:15; *koinōnia* 1:5; *synkoinōnous* 1:7) by supporting him during his affliction (*thlipsei* 4:14; *thlipsin* 1:17) for the sake of that gospel (1:16) as a factual example of such sharing. What was the Philippians' gift to Paul?

To even consider the possibility that it could have been a gift in kind, monetary or otherwise, is highly improbable given Paul's stand on this matter, which he iterates time and again in his letters (1 Cor 9:1-18; 1 Thess 2:9; 4:11; 2 Thess 3:7-9): he preaches the gospel free of charge. If one adds that (1) he is doing the same in this context (Phil 4:11-13) and (2) in the verse immediately preceding this passage he is giving himself as an example for the Philippians to follow (v.9), the suggestion of monetary or material gifts becomes totally unacceptable. The only remaining solution is to consider the sending of Epaphroditus as the "gift" Paul has graciously accepted. Earlier, Epaphroditus is referred to as their "apostle" (*apostolon*; sent) and "liturg" (*leitourgon*) to their "need" (*khreias*) (2:25). Here, we hear that the Philippians "sent" (*epempsate*;[6] 4:16) —whatever

---

[6] The verb *pempō* has the same meaning as *apostellō* which is from the same root as *apostolon* (sent; apostle).

they sent—to supply for Paul's "need" (*khreian*) (4:16) with Epaphroditus. Whatever was "sent" was received by Paul as "a fragrant offering, a sacrifice acceptable and pleasing to God" (4:18), which is liturgical terminology. Earlier Paul used similar liturgical terminology to refer to the expression of the Philippians' trust in his preaching to them the "word of life":

> Do all things without grumbling or questioning, that you may be blameless and innocent, children of God without blemish in the midst of a crooked and perverse generation, among whom you shine as lights in the world, holding fast the word of life, so that in the day of Christ I may be proud that I did not run in vain or labor in vain. Even if I am to be poured as a libation upon the sacrificial offering of your faith, I am glad and rejoice with you all. Likewise you also should be glad and rejoice with me. (2:14-18)

Not only is a reference to "joy" made in conjunction with Epaphroditus (I am the more eager to send him, therefore, that you may rejoice at seeing him again, and that I may be less anxious. So receive him in the Lord with all joy; 2:28-29), but it also opens the passage we are discussing: "I rejoice in the Lord greatly that now at length you have revived your concern for me." (4:10)

Can one be more precise as to the sense in which Epaphroditus is to be considered as the Philippians' gift to Paul? I believe one can. Towards the end of the passage Paul says: "I have collected (*apekhō*) full payment, and even in abundance; I am fulfilled (*peplērōmai*), having accepted (*dexamenos*) from (*para*) Epaphroditus the gifts that are from (*para*) you, a fragrant offering, a sacrifice acceptable (*dektēn*)[7] and pleasing to God. And my God will fulfill (*plērōsei*) every need (*khreian*) of yours

---

[7] From the same root as *dexamenos*.

according to his riches in glory in Christ Jesus." (4:18-19) From this passage, one gets the distinct impression of a liturgical action whereby Paul functions as the high priest (or bishop) who ✗ receives at the hands of (*para*) the deacon Epaphroditus the offering made by the hands of (*para*) the Philippians.[8] Furthermore, Paul repeatedly uses the term *logon* (word) in conjunction with the Philippians' gift, recalling the *logikēn latreian* (logic-al [word-y] worship) of Romans 12:1, and also bringing to mind its earlier use in conjunction with the same liturgical action referred to above: "holding fast to (*epekhontes*)[9] the word of life ... Even if I am to be poured as a libation upon the sacrificial offering of your faith, I am glad and rejoice with you all." (Phil 2:17-18) Thus, what the Philippians are sharing (*koinōnia*) with Paul is their trust in the message he has offered them. This is what he is accepting from them and then offering it to God who alone fulfills both his need and theirs. It is in this sense that Paul writes:

> And you Philippians yourselves know that in the beginning of the *gospel*, when I left Macedonia, no church entered into partnership (*ekoinōnēsen*) with me in the *matter* (*logon*)[10] of *giving* (*doseōs*) and receiving except you only; for even in Thessalonica you sent me help once and again. Not that I seek the *gift* (*doma*);[11] but I seek the *fruit*[12] which increases to your credit (*logon*). (vv.15-17)

---

[8] This seems actually to account for the mention of bishops and deacons at the beginning of the letter (1:2).

[9] From the same root as *apekhō* in 4:18.

[10] In Paul this term stands for his "gospel."

[11] From the same root as *doseōs*.

[12] As in 1:11.

The wordplay afforded by the term *logon* is linked to the fact that it means "account" (as in "render account of")[13] and it reflects that the Philippians as well as Paul must render account in conjunction with the "word": he inasmuch as he preached it, and they insofar as they put their trust in it. This is precisely what the Apostle spoke of earlier:

> Convinced of this, I know that I shall remain and continue with you all, for your progress and joy in the faith, so that in me *you may have ample cause to boast in Christ Jesus.* (1:25-26)

> Do all things without grumbling or questioning, that you may be blameless and innocent, children of God without blemish in the midst of a crooked and perverse generation, among whom you shine as lights in the world, holding fast the word of life, *so that in the day of Christ I may boast* that I did not run in vain or labor in vain. (2:14-16)

It is important to read Philippians 4:10-20 in light of the preceding comments. The Philippians had already expressed the eagerness to revive their concern for Paul, but had no opportunity to do so. "Reviving" points to an earlier expression of concern relating to the Philippians' seeing to Paul's need while he was in Thessalonica (4:16). Given the large distance between Philippi and Ephesus when compared to the short "hop" between Philippi and Thessalonica, it was indeed a sacrifice on the part of the Philippians to send Epaphroditus, one of their main leaders, to tend to the needs of the imprisoned Paul in Ephesus, for in doing so, they bereaved themselves of Epaphroditus for a long time.

---

[13] See for instance "Turn in (render; *apodos*) the account (*logon*) of your stewardship, for you can no longer be steward" (Lk 16:2).

Yet, for Paul, it is the Philippians who have the real "need," which will be fulfilled (*plērōsei*) at the coming of the Christ Jesus in glory (v.19). Thus their offering is wanting (*hysterēma*; 2:30), since they are still living and they have to continue on that path (on their way to the Kingdom) by remaining faithful to the gospel until their death. As for Paul, he does not experience such "want" (*hysterēsin*; 4:11). What appears to be want is, as in the case of Christ (*etapeinōsen heavton*; 2:8), a self-humbling on Paul's part. Indeed, as a counterpart to "abound" (*perissevein*) Paul uses once "abase oneself (be abased)" (*tapeinousthai*) and once "be lacking" (*hystereisthai*): "I know how to be abased (*tapeinousthai*), and I know how to abound (*perissevein*); in any and all circumstances I have learned the secret of facing plenty and hunger, abundance (*perissevein*) and want (*hystereisthai*)." (4:12) It is the same God who showed his power (*dynamis*) in his raising Christ (3:10: see also Rom 1:4) who empowers (*endynamounti*; Phil 4:13) Paul toward a similar goal (3:10-11). For the time being Paul is undergoing the necessary[14] tribulation (*thlipsei*; 4:14; see also 1:17) leading to that end. The Philippians are doing well to "have partnership" in it with him (*synkoinōnēsantes*; 4:14) since it is part of what the "grace of the gospel" entails, the grace in which they had decided to be his partners (*synkoinōnous*; 1:17).

The harking back to Philippians 1 is corroborated in the following verses where Paul not only takes up the notion of partnership but utilizes a vocabulary reminiscent of the beginning of the letter:

---

[14]See the use earlier of this idea of necessity in conjunction with the sacrifices he has to endure for the sake his apostolic activity: Phil 1:27 (But to remain in the flesh is more necessary on your account) and 2:25 (I have thought it necessary to send to you Epaphroditus my brother and fellow worker and fellow soldier, and your messenger and minister to my need).

And you Philippians yourselves know that in *the beginning of the gospel*, when I left Macedonia, no church entered into *partnership* with me in giving and receiving except you only; for even in Thessalonica you sent me help once and again. Not that I seek the gift; but I seek the *fruit* which increases to your credit. I have received full payment, and even *abound* in everything; I am *filled*, having received from Epaphroditus the gifts you sent, a fragrant offering, a sacrifice acceptable and pleasing to God. And my God will *fulfill* every need of yours according to his riches in *glory* in Christ Jesus. To our God and Father be *glory* for ever and ever. Amen. (4:15-20)

... thankful for *your partnership in the gospel* from *the first day* until now ... And it is my prayer that your love may *abound* more and more, with knowledge and all discernment, so that you may approve what is excellent, and may be pure and blameless for *the day of Christ*, *filled* with the *fruits* of righteousness which come through Jesus Christ, to the *glory* and praise of God. (1:5, 9-11)

What about the meaning of the phrase "the beginning of the gospel" in Philippians 4:15-16: "And you Philippians yourselves know that in the beginning of the gospel (*en archē tou evangeliou*), when I left (*exēlthon*; exited, went out of) Macedonia, no church entered into partnership with me in giving and receiving except you only; for even in Thessalonica you sent me help once and again"? This statement seems to go "against the grain," so to speak. The *archē* (basis, origin, principle) of the gospel seems to have begun upon Paul's leaving the Roman province Macedonia, after having preached there in two of its major cities, Philippi and the capital Thessalonica. How is that to be understood when the general assumption is that he *carried* and *brought* the gospel to the Gentiles?[15] It would behoove us to start our investigation with another text,

---

[15] See e.g. Acts 9:15; Rom 1:13-15; 15:23-24; Gal 1:16; 2:8.

interestingly occurring in a letter addressed to the other Macedonian church, where Paul states that he *was evangelized*, that is, *received the gospel message*:

> Therefore when we could bear it no longer, we were willing to be left behind at Athens alone, and we sent Timothy, our brother and *God's servant in the gospel of Christ, to establish you in your faith and to comfort you*, that no one be moved by these afflictions. You yourselves know that this is to be our lot. For when we were with you, we told you beforehand that we were to suffer affliction; just as it has come to pass, and as you know. For this reason, when I could bear it no longer, I sent *that I might know your faith, for fear that somehow the tempter had tempted you and that our labor would be in vain*. But now that Timothy has come to us from you, and *has evangelized us* (with the news) *your faith and love* and reported that you always remember us kindly and long to see us, as we long to see you—for this reason, brethren, in all our distress and affliction *we have been comforted* about you *through your faith*; for now *we live, if you stand fast in the Lord*. (1 Thess 3:1-8)

From this text it appears, just as Paul aptly wrote in Philippians, that the gospel is a "give and take" matter (4:15). The reason is that the "fruit" which is the seal of the gospel's effectiveness is always God's work, whether one is looking at the apostle or at his hearers:

> What then is Apollos? What is Paul? Servants through whom you believed, as the Lord assigned to each. I planted, Apollos watered, but God gave the growth. So neither he who plants nor he who waters is anything, but only God who gives the growth. He who plants and he who waters are equal, and each shall receive his wages according to his labor. For we are God's fellow workers; you are God's field, God's building. (1 Cor 3:5-9)

> Therefore, my beloved, as you have always obeyed, so now, not only as in my presence but much more in my absence, work out

your own salvation with fear and trembling; for God is at work in
you, both to will and to work for his good pleasure. (Phil 2:12-13)

And since everyone "receives," including the apostle who
ultimately is granted and entrusted with what he imparts (Rom
1:5; 1 Cor 2:12; 3:10; 4:1-5; 1 Thess 2:4), the gift (grace) of the
gospel remains a gift. Put otherwise, the apostle is to perceive the
fruit of his labor as a gift from God who alone "is at work in the
hearers" and "gives the growth to the planting of the apostle."
Consequently, the news that his labor bore fruit is an *evangelion*
(gospel, good news) for Paul. The gospel is not gospel unless the
word communicated by the evangelizer has been accepted as the
word of God himself by at least one of its hearers, and such
acceptance is nothing less than the "work" of God himself as
well. The evangelizer is always in a state of thanksgiving. One
cannot put this reality of the matter in more eloquent terms than
Paul himself:

> And we also thank God constantly for this, that when you *received*
> the word of God which you *heard from us*, you *accepted* it not as
> the word of men but as what it really is, *the word of God*, which is
> *at work* in you believers (*pistevousin*; who are trusting in this word.
> (1 Thess 2:13)

The conclusion imposes itself. As Isaiah taught (Is 40-55) that
God's eschatological messenger was to *evangelize* God's
instruction (*torah*; law) not only to the lost sheep of Israel but
also to the nations, this mission would not be fully carried out
unless at least one Jew of the diaspora and one Gentile living in
that same diaspora have accepted such *evangelization*. Put
otherwise, unless the gospel that is commissioned is received as
such, there would be no proof that it has been a gospel
(*evangelion*; good news). The quintessential Gentile is a Roman
citizen living in the land of Alexander of Macedon who opened

the way for Roman colonization of Syria and Mesopotamia, the land of nascent Judaism. The Macedonian Philippi was such a quintessential Roman colony, a mini-Rome.[16] As such it functioned as a symbol, and when one Philippian submitted to Paul's preaching, it was perceived as the realization of the Isaianic "gospel" and thus the *arkhē tou evangeliou*.

Having gone full circle Paul brings the letter to an end by inviting the Philippians to proceed, under Epaphroditus' leadership, on the "way" they started on even after his demise. As for him, he will remain their high priest, offering to God the due thanksgiving.

Vv. 21-23 ²¹Ἀσπάσασθε πάντα ἅγιον ἐν Χριστῷ Ἰησοῦ. ἀσπάζονται ὑμᾶς οἱ σὺν ἐμοὶ ἀδελφοί. ²²ἀσπάζονται ὑμᾶς πάντες οἱ ἅγιοι, μάλιστα δὲ οἱ ἐκ τῆς Καίσαρος οἰκίας. ²³Ἡ χάρις τοῦ κυρίου Ἰησοῦ Χριστοῦ μετὰ τοῦ πνεύματος ὑμῶν.

> *²¹Greet every saint in Christ Jesus. The brethren who are with me greet you. ²²All the saints greet you, especially those of Caesar's household. ²³The grace of the Lord Jesus Christ be with your spirit.*

Actually Paul is the high priest of all Gentiles (Rom 15:15-16). That is why, just as he does in his letter to the Romans, so here in his epistle to the believers of Philippi, he includes a greeting, including a kiss expressing brotherly love,[17] to each of the

---

[16] Philippi was a colony of veteran Roman soldiers.

[17] The verb *aspazō* (greet) used thrice in Phil 4:21-22 occurs in Rom 16:16 in conjunction with "a holy kiss" (*philēmati hagiō*); see also 1 Cor 16:20; 2 Cor 13:12; 1 Thess 5:26. This same holy kiss is said to be "the kiss of (brotherly) love" (*philēmati agapēs*) in 1 Pet 5:14. The closeness between Philippians and these other instances is at its clearest in 1 Thess 5:26 (Greet all the brethren with a holy [*hagiō*] kiss): both "brethren" and "holy (ones), saints" occur in Phil 4:21-22 (Greet every saint [*hagion*]

Philippians (4:21a), his helpers (v.21b), all those around him
(v.22). By adding "especially those of Caesar's household" Paul is
assuring the Philippians that the seed of the gospel has reached
not only the ears of that household (1:13), but has also taken
root in some of their hearts to the extent that the latter can join
in the kiss of peace as well as in table fellowship with the saints.
On the other hand, he is heralding to the community of
Philippi, mini-Rome, that the gospel was on its way to
conquering no less than Rome itself and, in this ultimate
conquest, the Philippians have already insured themselves full
partnership!

Having begun by wishing them continual grace and ultimately
the peace of the Kingdom (1:2), Paul bids them farewell with the
grace in which they stand now (Rom 5:2) with the hope that,
should they continue on this "way," they attain salvation and the
promised peace (5:1-11).

---

in Christ Jesus. The brethren who are with me greet you. All the saints [*hagioi*] greet
you, especially those of Caesar's household).

Further Reading

Commentaries and Studies

John Chrysostom, Homilies on Philippians in P. Schaff, ed., *The Nicene and Post-Nicene Fathers*. Grand Rapids, 1ˢᵗ Series, xiii 1979: 184-255.

Craddock, F.B. *Philippians*. Interpretation. Atlanta: John Knox Press, 1985. For pastors and teachers.

Das, A. A. *Paul, the Law, and the Covenant*. Peabody, MA: Hendrickson, 2001.

Fee, G. D. *Philippians*. IVP New Testament Commentary. Downers Grove, IL: InterVarsity Press, 1999. For pastors and teachers.

Fowl, S. E. *Philippians*. Two Horizons NT Commentary. Grand Rapids-Cambridge, UK: Eerdmans, 2005. An exegesis in conversation with theological concerns, trying to bridge the gap between biblical studies and systematic theology.

O'Brien, P. T. *The Epistle to the Philippians: A Commentary on the Greek Text*. The New International Greek Testament Commentary. Grand Rapids: Eerdmans, 1991.

Osiek, C. *Philippians, Philemon*. Abingdon New Testament Commentaries. Nashvilee, TN: Abingdon, 2000.

Martin, R. P. *A Hymn of Christ: Philippians 2:5-11 in Recent Interpretation & in the Setting of Early Christian Worship*. Downers Grove, IL: InterVarsity Press, 1997.

Martin, R. P. and Dodd, B. J., eds. *Where Christology began: Essays on Philippians 2*. Louisville: Westminster John Knox Press, 1998.

Peterlin, D. *Paul's Letter to the Philippians in the Light of Disunity in the Church*. Supplements to Novum Testamentum LXXIX. Leiden: E.J. Brill, 1995.

Reed, J. T. *A Discourse Analysis of Philippians: Method and Rhetoric in the Debate over Literary Integrity.* Journal for the Study of the New Testament Supplementary Series 136. Sheffield: Sheffield Academic Press, 1997.

Reumann, J. *Philippians.* The Anchor Yale Bible Commentaries. New Haven: Yale University Press, 2008.

Saunders, S. P. *Philippians and Galatians.* Interpretation Bible Studies. Louisville: Westminster John Knox Press, 2001.

Silva, M. *Philippians* (2nd ed.). Baker Exegetical Commentaries on the New Testament. Grand Rapids: Baker, 2005. Includes an excursus on scribal tendencies in the Pauline epistles.

Thurston, B.B. and Ryan, J. M. *Philippians and Philemon.* Sacra Pagina 10. Collegeville, MN; Liturgical Press, 2005.

Witherington III, B. *Friendship and Finanaces in Philippi: The Letter of Paul to the Philippians.* The New Testament in Context. Valley Forge, PA: Trinity Press International, 1994.

Wright, N. T. *Paul for Everyone. The Prison Letters. Ephesians, Philippians, Colossians and Philemon.* London: SPCK, 2002. Offers suggestions for the current relevance of Paul's teaching.

Articles

Carls, P. "Identifying Syzygos, Euodia, and Syntyche, Philippians 4:2f." *Journal of Higher Criticism* 8 (2001) 161-182. Opts for an allegorical, rather than historical individual, reading of these names.

Fowl, S. E. "Know Your Context. Giving and Receiving Money in Philippians." *Interpretation* 56 (2002) 45-58

Pretorius, E. "Role Models for a Model Church: Typifying Paul's Letter to the Philippians." *Neotestamentica* 32 (1998) 547-571

Snyman, A. H. "A Rhetorical Analysis of Philippians 1:1-11." *Acta Theologica* 24 (2005) 81-104. The passage is already part of the argumentation and not preparatory for the letter's arguments.

Snyman, A. H. "A Rhetorical Analysis of Phil 1:27-2:18." *Verbum et Ecclesia* 26 (2005) 783-809. Paul's intention is to invite his hearers to proclaim and live the gospel.

Thompson, A. J. "Blameless Before God? Philippians 3:6 in Context." *Themelios* 28 (2002) 5-12.

Verhoef, E. "Σύζυγος in Phil 4:3 and the Author of the 'We-sections' in Acts," *Journal of Higher Criticism* 5 (1998) 209-219. Σύζυγος is Luke who was a Philippian citizen.

CPSIA information can be obtained at www.ICGtesting.com
Printed in the USA
LVOW07s0008160216

475257LV00001B/78/P